LAWRENCE JOSEPH

CODES, PRECEPTS, BIASES, AND TABOOS

LAWRENCE JOSEPH was born in Detroit. He was educated at the University of Michigan, Cambridge University, and the University of Michigan Law School. His most recent book of poems is *Into It*. He is also the author of *Lawyerland*, a book of prose. He is a professor of law at St. John's University School of Law and also has taught in the Council of the Humanities and Creative Writing Program at Princeton University. Married to the painter Nancy Van Goethem, he lives in New York City.

CODES, PRECEPTS, BIASES, AND TABOOS

CODES, PRECEPTS, BIASES, AND TABOOS

POEMS 1973-1993

(LAWRENCE JOSEPH)

FARRAR,

STRAUS

AND

GIROUX

NEW YORK

FARRAR, STRAUS AND GIROUX
18 West 18th Street, New York, NY 10011

Printed in the United States of America
First edition, 2005

Grateful acknowledgment is made to *Boulevard*, *Broadsheet* (Cambridge, England), *Commonweal*, *Detroit Free Press*, *Epoch*, *The Kenyon Review*, *Michigan Quarterly Review*, *New Letters*, *New York Quarterly*, *Ontario Review*, *The Paris Review*, *Partisan Review*, *Pequod*, *Ploughshares*, *Poetry*, *Poetry East*, *Round & Catch*, *Stand*, *Verse*, and *Witness*, where poems in this book originally appeared. *Shouting at No One* was first published in 1983 by the University of Pittsburgh Press. *Curriculum Vitae* was first published in 1988, also by the University of Pittsburgh Press. *Before Our Eyes* was first published in 1993 by Farrar, Straus and Giroux.

Library of Congress Control Number: 2005927594
ISBN-13: 978-0-374-12517-2
ISBN-10: 0-374-12517-1

Designed by Gretchen Achilles

www.fsgbooks.com

P1

FOR NANCY VAN GOETHEM

CONTENTS

SHOUTING AT NO ONE

I was appointed the poet of heaven.

It was my duty to describe
Theresa's small roses
as they bent in the wind.

I tired of this
and asked you to let me
write about something else.
You ordered, "Sit
in the trees where the angels sleep
and copy their breaths
in verse."

So I did,
and soon I had a public following:

Saint Agnes with red cheeks,
Saint Dorothy with a moon between her fingers
and the Hosts of Heaven.

You said, "You've failed me."
I told you, "I'll write lovelier poems,"
but, you answered,
"You've already had your chance:

you will be pulled from a womb
into a city."

I

THEN

Joseph Joseph breathed slower
as if that would stop
the pain splitting his heart.
He turned the ignition key
to start the motor and leave
Joseph's Food Market to those
who wanted what was left.
Take the canned peaches,
take the greens, the turnips,
drink the damn whiskey
spilled on the floor,
he might have said.
Though fire was eating half
Detroit, Joseph could only think
of how his father,
with his bad legs, used to hunch
over the cutting board
alone in light particled
with sawdust behind
the meat counter, and he began
to cry. Had you been there
you would have been thinking
of the old Market's wooden walls
turned to ash or how Joseph's whole arm
had been shaking as he stooped
to pick up an onion,
and you would have been afraid.
You wouldn't have known
that soon Joseph Joseph would stumble,
his body paralyzed an instant
from neck to groin.
You would simply have shaken your head
at the tenement named "Barbara" in flames
or the Guardsman with an M-16
looking in the window of Dave's Playboy Barbershop,

then closed your eyes
and murmured, This can't be.
You wouldn't have known
it would take nine years
before you'd realize the voice howling in you
was born then.

DRIVING AGAIN

Driving again,
this time Van Dyke Avenue.
Just beyond my window
October wind raises
a leaf from a sewer,
a gray-haired man standing in a crowd
before the Mount Zion Temple
tips his hat, "Not bad, and you?"
When I was a child
I saw this church through the window
of a '51 Chevrolet
huddled beside my grandmother
in the backseat, her small
soft hands holding mine,
her perfume and the smell from squirrel
fur around her neck
spinning me to sleep.
Now I pass a woman,
her brown-blond face spotted purple,
who lowers her head
to spit, I see
a boy's words, "Dirty Killer Hood,"
in spray paint
on the wall of UAW Local 89.
Where was it? I stumbled
through the darkness to the door
before I realized
I was waking from a dream
of this street, this smoke
from Eldon Axle foundry, these
motor blocks stacked against
this dull sky. Too many times
I stood on a loading dock
and watched morning air change
from red to iron.

"Gimme coffee, gimme a cigarette,"
a face asked me, "ain't no life,"
another warned.
Here is the cemetery.
Beneath stones engraved in Arabic
my grandfather, my grandmother.
Beneath this earth
Grandpa whose sad eyes
could not endure
the pain of legs numbed
forever, Grandma
who smiled although cells
crushed her brain.
Years ago, on a day like this,
I fell to my knees
with my father to pull grass
from their stones.
I did not cry.
When I closed my eyes I did not pray.
Now, in a car, on Van Dyke,
I cry for them and for me.

I HAD NO MORE TO SAY

The last time I saw her
this flat
above the 7-Up Cadillac Bar—
empty now, windows closed
and covered with dust—
was a coffeehouse
to which I came
because I knew she'd
be there.
At the window, away
from the others,
she told me about
her mother, always
alone, her father
somewhere else,
in a hotel, in a bar,
her sister who hated
everything.
I told her about
Dodge Truck.
How I swung differentials,
greased bearings,
lifted hubs to axle casings
in 110° heat.
How the repairman said nothing
as he watched me
almost lose two fingers.
Although she did
not answer, her face
tensed and her eyes
told me, Don't
be afraid, it
won't last forever.
I had no more to say.
I took her hand,

walked to the center
of the room. As voices
on the phonograph sang
we turned, descended
in one beat, rose,
shifted and shifted again.
I sang to her
like the song.
I forgot
what the morning
would bring: the early
bus ride, nervousness,
the factory.

HERE

Pockets puffed with bottles,
hair stiff, rising
in gray wind.
He comes to a dog without hair
sleeping in the weeds
near the old Packard plant,
reads "can't see"
in the dust of a window.
One April morning as
spiders walk on soft, black stones
and the colors of motor oil
spread in rainwater pools
I am where he is,
but I don't look him in the eyes,
I don't want to hold him and tell him yes
if he asks something.
Above us white smoke
drifts with large dark clouds
toward old Poletown,
where the houses are gone.
Now it is September
and I am there, between
the silhouette of broken fences
and weeds with yellow hair
seizing their own piece of buried sun.
Rain streams down my face,
a poplar breathes
over the only house I can see,
burned and gutted.
The only sign of human life
is the crashing sound
of a bottle thrown hard on cement,
east of this wasteland,
where the towers smoke.

BETWEEN US

What was his name?
Drank gin from
a used paper cup, wasn't
even break time yet.
Sitting on a Hi-Lo, his
muscled arms hung
over the wheel.

           Between us
white dust covered
with sulfur, the dream
of a farm.
"In a few years ought to have
five head of cattle
and a tractor."

Nine years and 283 miles
to the south side, the voices
in the Whole Truth Mission
singing gospel. "But I
came right here to
Mt. Elliott Street.
Wasn't no future
praisin' Jesus."

I THINK ABOUT THIGPEN AGAIN

I think about Thigpen again.
On the floor in an apartment
on Boston Boulevard, he knows
he's going to die.
I see the record of the criminal court.
Thigpen opens the door,
sees a gun in his face,
pleads, "I don't have
nothing to do with this!"
According to the pathologist
death was caused
by massive tissue destruction,
contusion and swelling of the brain.
In the county morgue
Thigpen's father whispered,
"That's my baby son."
And what must have been said after was,
"You the wrongest person
in the wrongest place,
the wrongest time, Thig."
That was eleven years ago.
Sixteen years ago he stuffed
a basketball into the face
of the Brother Rice forward
who called him a name, and we
went wild. I saw him
in Louis the Hatter's, downtown.
He pointed at my Stetson,
laughed, "You ain't ever
gonna look like a nigger."
Later, he wrote poems of babies
in frozen tenements,
garbage alive with maggots,
the love a woman makes,

the greasy riders with Detroit skin,
the toughest in the world.

He would be the poet of this hell.

That bullet slicing your brain
isn't poetry, Thigpen.

IT WILL RAIN ALL DAY

Breakfast at Buck's Eat Place;
a portrait of Henry Ford,
two eggs, hash browns,
sour coffee. Afterwards
I walk out on Vernor Avenue,
"looks like a river in the rain,"
the signs from small stores hanging
over the wet sidewalks like trees.
But rivers are not passed over
by a woman wearing a windbreaker
with flags sewn on both shoulders,
muttering to herself, head down,
or an unshaven man older
than he is, his body slanting
as if he's about to fall
headlong into a dream.
Neither looks at me waiting
at the light, in my car,
as windshield wipers eliminate
the stars of water.
Along the cemetery, poplars
look upward with thousands
of eyes into the rain
that comes down on hills of lime
and coal, reminding me of Metz,
but the wind
that lifted rhododendrons that April
isn't here with me. What
do I want, driving through streets
past bars where fifty-year-old
truck drivers sip whiskey
and don't feel like talking,
past houses where chimney smoke
reveals fires and rooms I will
never know? On Fort Street

I pass the bar with "Fight Poverty—
Drink & Dance" scrawled in white paint
across its windowless front,
and then a block-long building,
windows knocked in, wires ripped
from the walls, toilet bowls
covered with dirt and spiderwebs.
It will rain all day.
I see a large crane lifting
a railroad car, piles of bald tires,
the two towers of Saint Anne's
where, in a corner, there are crutches,
body braces, and letters written
to acknowledge miracles. I want
all this to come to an end
or a beginning, I want to look
into the black eyes of the lone woman
waiting for a bus and say
something, I want my memory
to hold this air, so I can make
the hills with white hair
and the clouds breaking into blackness
my own, carry them with me
like the letters and icons
immigrants take in suitcases
to strange countries.

BEFORE GOING BACK

Shot five times in the chest
with a .38, only a boy,
member, the Black Killers gang,
on the table in the Emergency Room,
drugged, gasping, tube rammed
through his windpipe for ventilation.
Tube through which you breathed
for him after you cracked
and spread his chest with a knife
and bone cutters, cross-clamped
the descending aorta, held
and massaged his heart,
oversewed holes in the right ventricle
and holes at the hilum
of the lung and tied his chest
with yards of silk, blood
on your face and hands
and hair, blood soaked
through socks and shoes before
it rushed down the drain.
Now you pace the Receiving Dock,
breathe the hot July air,
its trace of sulfur, hear its sirens
coming toward you.
You shake your head to shake
away your headache. You don't
ask why you remember the man
your father said was "down
on his luck," his face fallen,
two overcoats opened
to frozen wind, his arm lifted
to announce words only he hears,
or why you remember the night
you got out of your car,
walked through the small crowd

outside the liquor store
just because, you thought later,
you needed to walk by them all
without looking any of them
in the eye or speaking,
you don't think "must
be past midnight," because
it doesn't matter what
is remembered, it doesn't matter
what time it is. What matters
is the boy will live.
He'll waken, his voice
hushed. You'll be the first one
to tell him he'll never talk again,
that he'll have to walk
with a cane. He'll cry. He'll
never know how you paced
this Dock before going back
to wipe sweat from his forehead
and whisper words he didn't hear.

NOT YET

When my father breathed
unevenly I breathed
unevenly, I prayed
in Saint Maron's Cathedral
for the strength
of a cedar tree
and for the world to change.
When I saw my father's tears
I did not pray;
I hated our grocery store
where the bullet
barely missed his heart,
I hoped the mists exhaled
by the Vale of Esk
in a country of lakes
four thousand miles away
would be mine.
That was before
Lopez whispered through his rotten teeth
behind a maze of welding guns,
"You're colored, like me,"
before I knew
there is so much
anger in my heart,
so much need
to avenge the holy cross
and the holy card
with its prayers for the dead,
so many words
I have no choice to say.
Years without enough to make me
stop talking!
I want it all.

I don't want
the angel inside me, sword in hand,
to be silent.
Not yet.

II

THE PHOENIX HAS COME TO A MOUNTAIN IN LEBANON

I
I was a child when the wolves came
from the north and ate our donkey.
My father shouted so much
I was afraid. I hid
in the heavy mountain grass
where he could not see me.
When it was dark I went back to the house.
He was not there.
My mother was on her knees
praying before the bag of silkworm eggs
that hung from the ceiling.

2

I was the kind of boy who prayed
before a statue's face,
sorry for all the tears
that were for me
because I was "always
inside out."

Again and again
I climbed above the village
to think about
what obsessed me:
the tax collectors who melted
the iron points of our plows
into guns, the shrapnel
I saw in my cousin's stomach;
to repeat to myself
what my brother's letter said—
"it is better here,
there is work, there is money
in these factories."

3

I stand over a dead body
and feel nothing
for the bones I've crushed:
my bones have been
crushed for centuries.
I fire my rifle into the sun,
shout God's name,
return to ruins to roast a lamb.
I will eat the head
first and then the bowels.
I will drink wine
until I cannot
see the dream of my own land.

4

The Phoenix has come
to a mountain
in Lebanon, its red flesh
breathing the sun,
breathing myrtle and poppies,
the prayers and wailing,
breathing the singing
Dog River and the Bridge
of Stone.
The Phoenix
is dying
and has come to be
what the land is,
wanting the eyes that no longer
listen, the widow's hair
on fire, wanting the stars
that do not touch
the stones.
The winds are dry
and do not
cool its burning;
the rains will not be
its new blood now.
Filled with the final words
of those left in a ditch
to die, with the black skin
of the bald woman
who's cried almost every day
for eighty years,
filled with the river at whose mouth
a thousand wars began,
river gone now into rock
and crystal after giving

the world its wheat,
the Phoenix
breathes,
goes down the mountain
to the burning cities,
to the sea
where a long boat waits to sail
to another world.

YOU ONLY EXIST INSIDE ME

Where Dix Highway ends
long boats tug ore
across a green canal.
In a café, Yemenites
cheat at dice
and talk about whores.
You drink coffee,
smoke, remember
a room, a table
that held the weight
of your elbows,
the small notebook
in which you wrote
"our labor put the world on wheels";
one day someone
will find it and think
of thick-lipped buckets,
iron pigs growing
into billets.
Alone, I walk this street
of ice, making this up:
you only exist inside me.
A siren blows.
It is 3:30.
I remember how
I punched the clock.
My legs jerked into full stride
toward a room.
I sat at a table
rubbing my eyes.

I did not feel.
I did not think.

LOUIE, SON OF HANNA FRANCIS

Catches the bus
at the corner
of Seminole and Charlevoix,
takes it past
the smell of bread, grinding
dynamos, yellow
streetlight,
Our Lady of Redemption
Melchite Catholic Church,
transfer
north at McDougall,
transfer downtown at
Gratiot, get off
at Russell, not yet
six o'clock,

Louie,
son of Hanna Francis,
descendant of Sem,
of the land Aram Naharaim
where, between two rivers,
soil is soft and black, good
for tomatoes, eggplant, corn,

says to himself, Buy
sausage from Hammond-Standish,
buy produce, but
no cauliflower, from
Caramagno, as he
walks in dark
drops of water dissolving
on his sun-colored face.

ENCOUNTER

Face lowered in his collar,
he leans back
against the darkness
of a boarded doorway.
A flame larger
than the sun
pours from a thin pipe.
Miles of factory
heaped to the half red
and half black sky
glow in his thin eyes.

       He steps out
into the frozen wind,
the only strip of light
breaks, scatters
behind him down the alley.
Says he knows
everything: the mysteries
of motors, how to get
easy jobs in the shop,
numbers, the streets,
where you can go
under a bridge at night
in a small boat, unnoticed.

FOG

All day the air was fog;
couldn't see
the barbed wire, rusting
scraps, stacks
and stacks of pallets,
the tar paper roof
of Dreamer's shack,
the underground
caverns of salt hardening
around bones.

              The fog says,
Who will save
Detroit now?
A toothless face
in a window shakes No,
sore fingers
that want to be still
say, Not me.
Not far away from where
Youmna lies
freezing in bed,
rolling her eyes, declaring,
This is a place!
the remains of mountains
wait to be moved
through smokestacks
into air.

ALL DAY

At four in the morning
already walking
up Orleans
to Eastern Market, two,
three miles away,
a burlap bag
over his shoulder,
the rows of wooden houses
asleep. Behind
him, low horns
on the river, a full moon
casting moist
blue light; ahead, the sounds
of cars and trucks
on Vernor Highway;
above, oak branches
turning in the high winds.

All day he drops the silver
into a cigar box;
the pennies he puts
in a jar. He gives
too much credit
and the markings on
small, torn pieces
of paper bag will be
forgotten. At dusk
he fills the bag again—
with eggplant, squash,
the last pieces of shank—
and goes
to the houses he knows
don't have enough,
saying nothing

as he gives, shaking his head
if someone starts to speak.

When the bag is empty
he walks
through the black streets
past faces rocking
on the porches. The shouts
of the children in the alley
and he's home, to Mary,
Katherine, Anne, Matry,
Isabelle, Sabe, Josephine,
Helen, Genevieve, Basily,
and Barbara. The screen door
slams behind him.
Unnoticed, he sits down
to unlace his shoes,
to rub his sore feet.
He leans back, his eyes
close, his head
begins to nod at the voices
in the kitchen; he sees,
a world away,
the salamander sliding
down a rock, stars
dropping behind mountains
into the sea.

HE IS KHATCHIG GABOUDABIAN

I

He hears screams in the alley:
a cousin cuts a cousin's throat.
"We are all cousins," they say,
but they are not his cousins,
these black men from Yemen,
curved daggers cinched to their waists,
who kill for women.

He coughs, wakens suddenly.
Is this a dream? What time is it?
Noon? He lifts the shade:
it is past noon; the smoke
from the plant is heavy, red,
the day is gray again.
He walks across his room,
lights a cigarette, sits down on the bed,
gets up, walks, sits down again.
His legs hurt; doctor says
his blood is bad. What time is it?
He's hungry. He scratches his ribs.
He must not forget to take his pills.

2
Before he is born
because there is no work in Sivas
his father crosses the border
into Bulgaria forever.
War brings soldiers with long rifles
who take his mother, brothers,
and sister away forever.
In Arabkir he is an orphan among orphans,
in Detroit an uncle sends him money
to come tap the cupola, pour
liquid metal into the ladle.

When I heard about their bodies
floating in a river of blood
you might say my heart was broke.
I was lost, there was no one
to tell me I was lost.
I used to pray beneath the cross
before I thought of all this,
before I thought.

3

He doesn't know how old he is,
he doesn't know his real name.

He knows pain crosses his shoulders.
His lungs cough blood.
He is dying.

He can't eat because he doesn't have
teeth and his gums bleed.
His room in the Hotel Salina doesn't have
heat and the pipes freeze
like the water in the toilet down the hall.

He complains to whomever listens
or doesn't listen
or to himself
if there is no one to complain to.

He is a well-known
loser at *barbouda*, a socialist
who speaks with arms and elbows.
He's ashamed to say he's sacrificed
women and family
to serve two masters: Henry Ford and dice.

4

The warm white wind, the afternoon light
feel the face of the man who knows he is dying.

His legs don't hurt as much.
He inhales without coughing.

A newspaper, sunglasses, a pack of cigarettes,
a hat, the clothes on his back,
a chair by a table in a coffeehouse, a window,
are his.
He can drink eight cups of coffee,
he can figure the importance
of Albania to Afghanistan.

This is where the world is!
Those who don't understand this don't understand!

He used to walk beside tons of sand,
storage bins, along the boat slip.
He remembers the dusk sun
golden across the black Rouge River.
He promises himself he will go there
one more time, one more time
to feel the power of earth, water, and sun
together, holding him.

5

In Salina, South Dearborn,
the air is cold, damp, deep
black and red, filled
with sulfur and the earth
roaring inside machines.
Crowds of young men on the street
shake and nod their heads,
waiting for the midnight shift.
If they do not acknowledge him
he does not care:
he is Khatchig Gaboudabian.
If he must shut himself in his room alone
he will.

I have the mind.
That will save me.

NOTHING AND NO ONE AND NOWHERE TO GO

I've laughed before no one,
cried before fire floating
in iron molds, felt
the crow and the peppergrass
against brown dawn.
I never pray "Father" or "Son,"
I scavenge if I have to.
At Hudson Motorcar
an Iraqi I worked with
never talked, except
after the shift began,
he'd kneel and sing
"Allah la ilah." He wanted
mercy, from somewhere
in Arabia, but I never
wanted anything
from the metal rushing
into sand troughs
or the grease
I smelled and breathed.
I've always waited:
for warm rain to wash the sky,
for the woman
beside the river of sludge
to disappear.
Now I wait for the hours left,
alone, shivering,
wait until I can't
hear myself talking to myself
or hear my heart beat
for nothing and no one
and nowhere to go.

III

STOP TALKING TO YOURSELF!

There is always steam pouring from manholes,
there are always smokestacks heaving poison.

There is a dog behind the "Chez Paree Hotel"
kicking its hind legs, foaming at the mouth.

On a porch with Doric columns, a boy spits
into the wind. He wears a Borsalino hat.

Hands in his coat pockets, he wants you to know
he carries a gun. Old man on Bellevue Street

who came here believing the Five Dollar Day,
no teeth, cigarette hanging from his lower lip,

opens a barbed wire gate before a stone mansion.
You hear your voice. You don't remember speaking.

Stop talking to yourself! Be disciplined!
Look away from Our Lady of Lourdes

appearing to a statue of Bernadette beside
the brick warehouse with "Baby Pimp Dog" painted

across its wall. Forget the Albanian gypsy
whose hatred you feel as you stare into her eyes.

Do as you always do to convince yourself: recite
the Our Father and Hail Mary out loud, in Latin.

THERE IS A GOD WHO HATES US SO MUCH

I

I was pulled from the womb
into this city.

I learned words when my grandfather
lost both legs.

Before the altar of God
I spent hours on my knees.
I felt God's anger
when my semen spilled into my hand.
I ate God's body.
I promised to never sin.

I learned sadness from my mother's eyes.
I learned silence in the dust
a woman hid behind
to cover her face of scars.
I learned blood from my father
fallen to a wooden floor,
a thief's bullet inside him.
He lived to warn me to forget.

After that I sucked darkness.

II
Years were a breath.

Alone, with whirring metal,
clattering and pounding
I could not abstract,
smells that tortured me,
I felt my words close inside me
like marrow.

I was a system of laws
I hated, a boy
afraid of burning
in a city that was burning
as my father cried
and my mother whispered in my hair.

III

I am the poet of my city.

I am the earth that burns the air,
those who talk to themselves,
blood and grease on hands.
I need to know
why I do not want to remember.

In dreams I run through streets
terrified, away
from mouths that hate me,
my face washed with fear.
In dreams I kill
so I will not be killed.

The city is the shadow
strapped to my back.

I am the poet of that shadow.

IV
Mother says, "Don't
think about it too much."

Father splashes cold water on his face,
vomits his nightmare:
he sweat before a man
who wanted to kill him.

I hold a holy candle and a palm branch,
kiss the feet of a statue,
drink holy water,
imagine my body without words,
pray to be able to sacrifice
like the saint
with arrows in his heart.

God gives the world
the brown and black frost
the city climbs through
to stars no one can see.

V

That is where I am now, in this city
where there are hours of sun
above the horizon and dirt in the air
that makes me want to holler.

There is a God who hates us so much:
we are given ears to hear ribs kicked in,
we are given eyes to see eyes close
before a city that burns itself to death.

Father shouts until his throat cracks,
the river stops in its sludge,
I pray to know what to pray for:
there is a God who hates us so much.

I was born in this city and live in this city
and know this city like no one else.
Who makes me eat my words and makes my eyes pain:
I measure you according to your creation.

IN THE TENTH YEAR OF WAR

I bend
over the machine. Heat
and oil
tune my inner ear. I'm
not ashamed, I
hang my head in
anticipation. Father,
steel smooth and silver,
make my brain new,
Jesus, the dirt on the walls
is coming from my body,
and love,
the spirit coming from your body—
everywhere you look now,
everything you touch,
it's good.
When,
in the tenth year of war
I prayed for help
and no one came,
I danced before the machine.

IS IT YOU?

Where the giant magnet lifts
pig iron and bales of steel
and a larva dangles
from a spider's thread
beside an old press machine,
where the '53 De Soto is
among piles of chassis
and transmissions,
and air is wakened
by an ore boat's horn,

someone calls.
Is it you? who numbers stars
the same as Job's
and hides words in my bones
demanding, Count them?
Is it you, calling me,
your blackest rib?

WHEN YOU'VE BEEN HERE LONG ENOUGH

You breathe yellow smoke, you breathe lead
beside the river, talking out loud to no one.

A rat slips by you into the cold green water.
No longer, at six o'clock Mass, do you kneel,

body bent over and swaying, chanting,
"Mea culpa, mea culpa, mea maxima culpa,"

offering your sorrow to the Poor Souls in Purgatory,
no longer do you dream of your mother as a child

waiting for a streetcar in the snow, praying
to Saint Jude to cure her sister's paralyzed hand.

When the waitress argues, "What you do is
hang them, downtown, in Grand Circus Park—

that would keep them off the streets," you don't answer.
You hear about the woman who twenty-five years ago touched

the back of your head and said, "It's shaped
just like your daddy's." She just sat there

and watched blood spray from her cut wrist all over
her room in the La Moon Manor Hotel. You just

shake your head. You're not surprised.
Because, when you've been here long enough

no one can make you believe the Black Cat
Dream Book provides your winning number.

Heaven answers your prayers with dust and you swallow it.
Alone, early morning, on the Wyoming Crosstown bus,

you feel the need to destroy, like everyone else,
as the doors open and no one comes on.

JUST LIKE YOU

Just like you
I hate
the boy with rotten teeth
who bites his lip, smiles,
"I didn't do it,"
just like you
I curse
my shit and want to dance
on the Board of Directors' oak table
in the Tower of Glass.
Bless me,
Father, for I have sinned:
I tell lies,
I don't pray.
I believe
the woman who shows me her artificial eye,
I prophesy
at noon gray sky will fall.
Just like you
burned earth burns my brain.
Not even a relic
touched to a relic
of the One True Cross
balances me.

IN EACH CELL OF MY BODY

When the world was born
I saw God
in the wind, with wings,
move into earth
and sleep.

In that life
I stared at mirages,
the roofs of shacks,
above them white water and sky,
Mama always saying, "That's
all he does."

In each cell of my body
is a morning: my sister
bleeds as she sleeps,
the old man comes home, arms
speckled with grease,
the scent of opening elm buds
hangs in the air,
and twenty-seven silver stacks
push smoke
under a sky of rain clouds.

DO WHAT YOU CAN

In the Church of I AM she hears there is a time to heal,
but her son, Top Dog of the Errol Flynn gang,

doesn't lay down his sawed-off shotgun,
the corn she planted in the field where

the Marvel Motor Car factory once was
doesn't grow with pigweed and cocklebur.

When someone in the Resurrection Lounge laughs,
"Bohunk put the two-foot dogfish in the whore's hand,"

someone's daughter whispers, "Fuck you,"
places a half-smoked cigarette in her coat pocket,

swings open the thick wooden door, and walks
into air that freezes when it hears frost

coming from Sault Sainte Marie. Driving, I see
a shed of homing pigeons, get out of my car to look.

I answer, "What you care?" to a woman who shouts, "What you
    want?"
Beside the Church of Saint John Nepomocene

an old man, hunched and cold, prays, "Mother of God"
to a statue of the Virgin Mary

surrounded by a heart-shaped rosary
of fifty-three black and six white bowling balls.

Where the Ford and Chrysler freeways cross
a sign snaps, 5,142,250,

the number of cars produced so far this year in America.
Not far away, on Beaufait Street,

a crowd gathers to look at the steam
from blood spread on the ice. The light red,

I press the accelerator to keep the motor warm.
I wonder if they know

that after the jury is instructed
on the Burden of Persuasion and the Burden of Truth,

that after the sentence of twenty to thirty years comes down,
when the accused begs, "Lord, I can't do that kind of time,"

the judge, looking down, will smile and say,
"Then do what you can."

EVEN THE IDIOT MAKES DEALS

On Mack Avenue the smell of hot iron closes your eyes:
you've chosen a city that moans in its dirt.

You memorize prayers in Arabic and forget them.
You memorize Statutes of Frauds and forget them.

You remember a boy with a knife who wanted money
from the Joseph Food Market safe. Sixteen years later

your uncle tells how he wakens, sweating, shaking,
"don't kill me," as the knife cuts his throat again.

He shows you the scar; it's healed.
"You learn how to forget," he reminds you.

You can't forget the boy who beats a woman to death
for money he could just have taken. His bones,

our bones, crumble in this damp, cold haze.
Even the idiot makes deals. She'll sell you her hair.

She wants you to look at her pocked face and her drool.
She knows you'll put a coin into her waiting hand.

IT'S NOT ME SHOUTING AT NO ONE

Before dawn, on the street again,
beneath sky that washes me
with ice, smoke, metal.
I don't want to think
the bullet pierced my shoulder,
the junkie's rotten teeth
laughed, his yellow hair froze.
I'm careful: I smoke
Turkish tobacco cigarette butts,
I drink a lot to piss a lot,
I fry the pig in its own fat,
eat the knuckles, brain, and stomach;
I don't eat the eyes!
Always four smokestacks
burning bones, somewhere
tears that won't stop,
everywhere blood becomes
flesh that wants to say something.
It's not me shouting at no one
in Cadillac Square: it's God
roaring inside me, afraid
to be alone.

CURRICULUM VITAE

Both in nature and in metaphor identity is
the vanishing-point of resemblance.

—WALLACE STEVENS

IN THE AGE OF POSTCAPITALISM

The disabled garment worker
who explains to his daughter
he's God the Holy Spirit
and lonely and doesn't care
if he lives or dies;
the secret sarcoma shaped like a flower
in the bowels of a pregnant woman;
ashes in the river, a floating chair,
long, white, shrieking cats;
the watch that tells Zurich,
Jerusalem, and Peking time;
and the commodities broker
nervously smiling, mouth slightly twitching
when he says to the police he's forgotten
where he left his Mercedes:
everything attaches itself to me today.
Thirty million—the American
Broadcasting Corporation World News
conservatively estimates—
murders already this century.
Whether the public debt
may have affected case history
Number 51's excuse that she was abandoned
on the pier by a dolphin
and the question "What Has Become of
the Question of 'I' "
are topics for discussion
at the Institute for Political Economy.
I know all about the transmigration of souls.
I know about love and about strife.
To delight in a measured phrase,
to bank the rage in the gut,
to speak more softly,
to waken at three in the morning to think only of her
—in the age of postcapitalism.

Yellow and gray dusk thickens around the Bridge.
Rain begins to slant between
the chimneys and the power plant.
I don't feel like changing,
or waiting anymore either,
and I don't believe we're dreaming
this October sixth, in New York City,
during the nineteen eighties.

MY EYES ARE BLACK AS HERS

Much did he see. Slowly
did he learn. Could not
realize himself significant
in a house of such magnitudes.

Mama held his tender awe.
She alone knew to touch,
sang to herself thoughts
of her own though never

did anyone listen but he.
He knew in her dresser
her powders and perfumes,
rose-colored creams.

He knew in her closets
stilled perfume of her dresses,
furs and silks and stockings,
the satin in the long cedar chest.

It was terribly hot—heat wave;
his patron saint's feast.
He said his prayers.
He said nine prayers:

Grandma and Grandma and Aunt Lila,
Aunt Adele, Mama, Aunt Ida,
and Aunt Jeanette—and God the Son,
and Mrs. Makdessi who has no one.

"This is a smart one," Mama says.
My eyes are black as hers.
"Too smart, I'm afraid—he'll
keep unhappy because of it,"

Mama said. I heard her.
That's what Mama said.
On the feast of my patron saint
that's what my mama said.

CURRICULUM VITAE

I might have been born in Beirut,
not Detroit, with my right name.
Grandpa taught me to love to eat.
I am not Orthodox, or Sunni,
Shiite, or Druse. Baptized
in the one true Church, I too
was weaned on Saint Augustine.
Eisenhower never dreamed I wore
corrective shoes. Ford Motor Co.
never cared I'd never forgive
Highland Park, River Rouge, Hamtramck.
I memorized the Baltimore Catechism.
I collected holy cards, prayed
to a litany of saints to intercede
on behalf of my father who slept
through the sermon at seven o'clock Mass.
He worked two jobs, believed
himself a failure. My brother
believed himself, my sister denied.
In the fifth grade Sister Victorine,
astonished, listened to me recite
from the Book of Jeremiah.
My voice changed. I wanted women.
The Jesuit whose yellow fingers
cracked with the stink of Camels
promised me eternal punishment.
How strange I was, with impure thoughts,
brown skin, obsessions.
You could tell by the way I walked
I possessed a lot of soul,
you could tell by the way I talked
I didn't know when to stop.
After I witnessed stabbings
outside the gym, after the game,
I witnessed fire in the streets.

My head set on fire in Cambridge,
England, in the Whim Café.
After I applied Substance and Procedure
and Statements of Facts
my head was heavy, was earth.
Now years have passed since I came
to the city of great fame.
The same sun glows gray on two new rivers.
Tears I want do not come.
I remain many different people
whose families populate half Detroit;
I hate the racket of the machines,
the oven's heat, curse
bossmen behind their backs.
I hear the inmates' collective murmur
in the jail on Beaubien Street.
I hear myself say, "What explains
the Bank of Lebanon's liquidity?"
think, "I too will declare
a doctrine upon whom the loss
of language must fall regardless
whether Wallace Stevens
understood senior indebtedness
in Greenwich Village in 1906."
One woman hears me in my sleep
plead the confusions of my dream.
I frequent the Café Dante, earn
my memories, repay my moods.
I am as good as my heart.
I am as good as the unemployed
who wait in long lines for money.

THIS IS HOW IT HAPPENS

This is how it happens, Paine
—says he's related in some way to Tom—

says, touching the moisture
on the side of his whiskey and ice.

The dollar declines, decreased
foreign investment. Consequently,

the deficit must be paid for
solely by Americans, crunching

the financial markets into inflation.
Interest rates exploding

while taxes rise! Expansion
never before so debt-ridden!

Expectations never so supreme.
Never have the happy been so well liked . . .

The day after Orpheus dies—
shot point-blank with a shotgun

by his father who, later questioned
whether he loved his son,

testified he couldn't say he disliked him—
the announcement of the latest fashion:

mink coats for men (Orpheus wore a tuxedo
at his press conference in Amsterdam

when, without hesitation,
he replied that his mission was to tell

about the upcoming holocaust
to whoever possessed the consciousness

to believe). And what about
that afternoon that August? Do you remember?

You worked in one room, through book
after book; two rooms away

she stretched a new canvas, the southern
light hot and almost red across her face

—who more alone, or afraid?—
whose desires or volitions

less inexorable to the other's?
And what about your first brush

with fame? Serving Mass
for Father Coughlin in his Shrine

years after he'd been silenced by the Pope
—Coughlin! eloquently

ranting on the nature of money,
the mercy of Christ Militant,

the Christian Corporate State,
the Satan of the Jewish question

not in the central bank of Berlin;
no one cared what you thought about him,

no one cares now. Do you see?
Your mother, silent, her life

a series of disappointments.
Do you remember the first time

you saw a man your own age collapse
on the street from hunger and weakness?

Let's just say now it was
intentional when your hand brushed

against her blouse—the subtle knowledge of
who touches whom with which meanings.

Let's say the darkening of your voice
combined with an ever-increasing

refined sense of phrasing creates
religious intensity. And who could change

your purpose? Speaking a different tongue
in the Park where the two rivers

merge, or else by the oak benches
in some Court of Equity, your gaze

almost balanced. From the Heights,
through the Bridge's rows of iron

woven and girded in a silhouetted loom,
a woman might be seen closing her eyes

to think, or perhaps, later, to cry;
a woman, exhausted and sorrowful, might know

she must put on her face and forget
what just went through her mind.

FACTORY RAT

Hands of the West Virginian who insists
you're a Greek hillbilly and hands of Jesse
who insists "Can't be all that bad
if you a son of David"; long, bone-fingered
hands of Milton, who wears his 57th
Infantry combat fatigues, and your hands
at General Motors Truck & Coach in 1967
sandpaper primered bodies.
Imitate Milton: cut the thumb
and forefinger from a glove.
Squirt the foreman's eyes bleed;
he's drunk—"Don't sand with that
half-assed glove on"—the same night
the psycho pushing bodies onto the line
doesn't look and catches your knees. Jones,
at break time, excited about the girl
younger than his daughter he meets
on Sunday in a bar on Wide Track Road.
Pee Wee, nearby, negotiates with Red,
suddenly opens his mouth, wiggles
his tongue, "They love it!"
The newspaper admits in July Pontiac burns
—do you want any trouble?
Forget the dust from the sandpapered primer
is flakes of metal. When Jesse
repeats "Hebrew!" and repeats
"What's the matter, Rabbi?" just smile.
When the relief man cheats cheat him back.
When you walk through the gate
you know the time. When a stranger asks
"Why's someone young as you work here?"
don't answer. You don't answer
when he answers "You're a factory rat like me."

I'VE ALREADY SAID MORE THAN I SHOULD

All that I know is that I know
my age from a face that was young

when I was, and is young no longer,
and the smell of salt from the East River

streaked black by black broken clouds
isn't mine to choose. When,

in the Hall of Oceanic Life, the waiter
brings medallions of veal, morels,

and wild rice pilaf from a serving plate
onto my plate, 410 glasses

await 1979 Chateau Chasse-Spleen,
and in the past my grandma

walks with two oak canes
beneath the street's great silver maples

to the house I lived in my first year.
When, in this morning's paper,

the renowned poet and critic
professor is quoted decrying

the demise of English forms,
I write Esquire after my name.

This isn't an apology. I read
Fadi is too young to read, but

the message seems to have gotten through:
he vows he will kill who killed

his father and crush the bones.
This isn't a credo or a confession.

I make favors, complain, wear
a white shirt and blue suit. I'm tired.

I see controversy continues whether
the current situation is civil

commotion or war. "Fifty thousand
to one hundred thousand killed, a wracked

government, an army in barracks,
howitzers, tanks!" the president

of the insurance association's
property division lashes out in reply.

It isn't for nothing that I deny
interior theological dialogue, doubt

the existence of the new aeon,
don't sleep past dawn anymore.

In the offices of the great firm
whose name might matter

I won't reveal what I abhor,
or my desire, if I can't be rich,

to be, instead, moral or famous.
In the Desbrosses Street café

I order my third cappuccino al cognac,
light another cigarette,

confide to whoever listens
I've already said more than I should.

THIS MUCH WAS MINE

Saturday morning, the June sun
already hot and white.
On the first tee,
Detroit Golf and Country Club,
the players, the caddies.
I am appointed Don Delaney's bag.
First, the bets:
one hundred dollars a nassau
five ways, automatic presses,
each player against the others.
Then, long drives lost
in the light and found
on the fairways, explosions
of grassblade and sand,
the quick roll and curve of the ball
from the apron onto the green.
On the eighteenth Delaney
asks how much club. I tell him,
he hits the 7-iron
perfectly, one putts,
wins a lot of money.
You've probably forgotten
the stories in the national newsmagazines
years ago about "Dice" Delaney.
"Dapper of dress, genial of manner,
loud of voice," he gained
his reputation at craps,
hustled golf, made
the largest independent book in America
before his luck ran out.
Although I saw wonder when I saw
how much could be won
with skill and with calculation,
I hated his nervous face, his eyes
without color that couldn't

be still, the broken laughter
he feigned as he counted
combinations of money in his head.
I stuffed the crisp ten dollar bill
he paid me into my pocket.
I knew where it came from.
I knew this much was mine.

BY THE WAY

What I saw was impossible
together. Only months between
the factories, furnaces
with hissing bronze pipes, smoke
streamed across flat skies,
and a woman named Mimi di Nescemi, who exits
in black silk trousers, delicate heels;
a man who says his name is Ra
wrapped in blankets in a cardboard box
on Gold Street. I tried to explain.

On February second, 1970,
at eight minutes past four
my father in his grocery store
perceived how desperate the man was
—he'd kill. The bullet missed
the spinal cord, miraculously,
the doctor said. Everything
eventually would be all right.
The event went uncelebrated among hundreds
of felonies in that city that day.

At lunch at the Broad Street Club
I couldn't stop looking at
the woman at the table across from me.
Beige-colored suit, blouse
unbuttoned two buttons, I could tell
she was sensual and smart and that
her presence hadn't gone unnoticed
by two bankers whose conversation
on floating exchange rates and computers
I couldn't help but overhear.

I couldn't help but overhear
my thoughts and opinions.

My starting point? Not Plato.
What if poverty and anger
and the desire for thrills,
and tribal attitudes, exist
not only on the streets but innately
—inherent, if you will,
within the boundaries of the nation,
social and economic classes, our time?

On public television, on a program
on national affairs, Mr. Getty
distinctly recalls his director's
emphasis: at one hundred dollars a share
or higher, the museum was a seller
not a buyer. "Which is a rhyme,"
Mr. Getty explains. "Put me among
the circle of poets for that.
That's the lowest circle
in Dante's hell, by the way."

In the Third Circle of Alexandria's
Department of Irrigation Services,
Special Clerk Constantine Kavafis
aggravated his imagination, thought
too much about the poet Lamon's
popularity (the rave of all
literary Beirut), and interpreted
the Asian blood in his veins.
In another circle, poets punctuate
their remarks with tics and odd sneezes.

In some circles, poets whip themselves
under every conceivable influence into mania
to advertise. In another room
a beautiful woman toward whom men always

try to be personal; which secrets,
which consciousness, cause her aloofness?
In the lowest circle in hell the Republic
has been betrayed, by the way.
In the lowest circle, shadows
seize skulls with their teeth.

IN THIS TIME

I

When you don't understand yet
the city's lungs are gray,
the shacks on wooden pillars,
salt heaps, scrap and cinders
breathe blood. When you can't
even imagine Grand River on fire.

When Czechlewski pronounces
"love is the mysterious
labyrinth that emanates
from the Divine." Your father
vomits every morning to ease
his nerves. Latin syllables
are counted, quantified.
Low blanket of yellow sky
inwardly summons prayer.

When you don't understand yet
the look in your face is fear.

II

In the Jesuit School
the middle voice
of the optative mood,
cassocks, wooden
kneelers, pages
of cosines, syllogisms.
In the imagination
the blue cotton skirt
at Immaculata High School
lifted with both hands.

In the Memorial Building
after the dance "when

the music begins to play
automatically you're
on your way." At home
the father returns late,
green work clothes
smeared with flesh
of animals he butchers.

III
It is blessed on Brush Street
beside the machine shop's junkyard
where hands are warmed
over fire in oil cans.
It is awesome, the poplar's shivering gold.
He is imitated, the soldier saint
who instructs that conversation,
if disordered, is sin.
She is praised whose tongue
opens your mouth in the damp basement.

It is enough sun behind blue smoke
to rent the elm buds, to burn the cloud's bloom.

IV
In this time a boy works
his mind beyond half dreams,
beyond the older woman alone
at midnight leaning toward him
from a windowsill, a thousand
chimneys hissing, the sudden
sweat from the April heat
broken down his backbone.

Already his heart
accepts its ceaseless weight.

STOP ME IF I'VE TOLD YOU

That year, too, was finished.
Yellow fog vanished

in the lane of spring mistletoe,
Byron's Pool, Newton's rooms.

Emphatically, emphatically she said no
the second from the last time.

Her hair was light, bright red and beautiful.
She cried, I said don't.

While, drugged, I increased
to a very high power,

several billion dollars of bombs
dropped on Cambodia. Jerolds,

on Jesus Green, declared
he intended to be great.

R.A.H. Prince, at High Table,
observed Lewis's subtle depiction

of Eliot's eyes in the famous portrait
that hung in Hall, insisted

every American owned a car.
Stop me if I've told you about

the treatise on evil in the University Library,
purple rhododendrons

burst apart in midnight sun,
Paris, Thonon-les-Bains, Geneva in April,

my sensitivity, and my luck.
Home in November after my second Michaelmas

to find—myself. Myself
an abstraction; myself

drives to see the great factories,
wills his desire not to accumulate

in the brain, remembers
the Angelus's cadences

on the Shrine of the Little Flower's chimes.
Have I told you about

the Pillar of Families and the Hope
of the Sick, instants

of awareness, my own words
I should not comprehend?

July, in the village Ajaltoun
in the mountain in Lebanon

on the feast of Saint Elias,
while Beirut's heavy moon

and tin and cardboard houses
revolved behind my eyes,

I danced one step forward
and, then, one step to the side,

knelt, rose straightbacked,
upright in the beginnings

of some strange knowledge
I thought was true.

I vowed discipline. I vowed love.
I read all the books, believed

my irony my nostalgia reversed—
I believed it. January

in Cambridge, a new year,
I waken at dawn to walk

to the old Gasworks outside the city
toward familiar smells.

MAMA REMEMBERS

I tried to do what I was told, made
the sign of the cross before icons
of the Apostles and my prayer equal
fat Father Riashi sweating, incanting

Syriac surrounded by incense smoke
in Our Lady of Redemption Melchite Church
my fifth Palm Sunday. Did I know
arteries hardened, the business

was changed by years of no money,
there was a miscarriage, in January,
on Thursday, in the kitchen, in 1951?
Grandpa, legless, appeared to me alone

in dazzling hot September afternoon.
Mama could not know how not to be sad.
In the sunroom before the picture window
Aunt Rose and Aunt Angele compared

the color of my skin to old Uncle Moise's.
There was enough silence to divide.
My brother did not tell what he knew,
took his share, whatever he could.

Did I believe Grandma's eyes revealed
her will to live or her need to die?
Mama remembers if my father ever cried.
Mama remembers how much she cried.

SAND NIGGER

In the house in Detroit
in a room of shadows
when Grandma reads her Arabic newspaper
it is difficult for me to follow her
word by word from right to left
and I do not understand
why she smiles about the Jews
who won't do business in Beirut
"because the Lebanese
are more Jew than Jew,"
or whether to believe her
that if I pray
to the holy card of Our Lady of Lebanon
I will share the miracle.
Lebanon is everywhere
in the house: in the kitchen
of steaming pots, leg of lamb
in the oven, plates of kousa,
hushwee rolled in cabbage,
dishes of olives, tomatoes, onions,
roasted chicken, and sweets;
at the card table in the sunroom
where Grandpa teaches me
to wish the dice across the backgammon board
to the number I want;
Lebanon of mountains and sea,
of pine and almond trees,
of cedars in the service
of Solomon, Lebanon
of Babylonians, Phoenicians, Arabs, Turks,
and Byzantines, of the one-eyed
monk, Saint Maron,
in whose rite I am baptized;
Lebanon of my mother
warning my father not to let

the children hear,
of my brother who hears
and from whose silence
I know there is something
I will never know; Lebanon
of Grandpa giving me my first coin
secretly, secretly
holding my face in his hands,
kissing me and promising me
the whole world.
My father's vocal cords bleed;
he shouts too much
at his brother, his partner,
in the grocery store that fails.
I hide money in my drawer, I have
the talent to make myself heard.
I am admonished to learn,
never to dirty my hands
with sawdust and meat.
At dinner, a cousin
describes his niece's head
severed with bullets, in Beirut,
in civil war. "More than
an eye for an eye," he demands,
breaks down, and cries.
My uncle tells me to recognize
my duty, to use my mind,
to bargain, to succeed.
He turns the diamond ring
on his finger, asks if
I know what asbestosis is,
"the lungs become like this,"
he says, holding up a fist;
he is proud to practice
law which "distributes

money to compensate flesh."
Outside the house my practice
is not to respond to remarks
about my nose or the color of my skin.
"Sand nigger," I'm called,
and the name fits: I am
the light-skinned nigger
with black eyes and the look
difficult to figure—a look
of indifference, a look to kill—
a Levantine nigger
in the city on the strait
between the great lakes Erie and St. Clair
which has a reputation
for violence, an enthusiastically
bad-tempered sand nigger
who waves his hands, nice enough
to pass, Lebanese enough
to be against his brother,
with his brother against his cousin,
with cousin and brother
against the stranger.

RUBAIYAT

All the stories about killing, burned bones, the smoke
from burning bones, a body tied by a rope fastened to a Mercedes
flying above the ground, cut-up body in a nylon bag,
black hoods, hallucinations, stylized hair and pure gold chains,

a report, according to the government official, forty-two
forced into the church and hacked to death with axes on the altar,
accounts confirmed by government officials, a five-year-old boy
discovered nailed to a doorway in the form of a cross.

And what do you think you're doing when you want the names
and the years of the history, who begot whom and who made
which flesh which words that hate for which particular reasons
that compel the pride of the horrors of the oppressed?

That's how the brain talks, evil in its wakefulness.
It's just too crazy and it's too much and not unreal.
Fourteen years it's been now since Beirut's dust and the Shouf's sun
repressed. The crippled child without eyelashes spoke.

His face blue, his words didn't leave his mouth—
this is twelve years before Corporal McMahon in the bunker
"The Psycho Ward" beside the airport below Souk-al-Gharb
pokes at his C-rations, answers back home he liked to hunt geese.

Uncle Shikory three times a week took a bus to Beirut.
He did some deals in the back of some store. Talked slowly
in French about how little he remembered his brother, my
        grandfather.
Angele, his daughter, frail and small, her husband dead ten years

—a cerebral hemorrhage. She wears layers of black.
He was only thirty-five and she isn't young. I hear her
weeping in the dark. Her eyes deep dark, sad and heavy.
She likes me—my moods. Once she touched my shoulders,

whispered, *d'accord, d'accord.* I've never forgotten that.
When I try consciously not to forget I surely will exhaust
the imagination. April. A year ago. In the Consul's residence.
Yasine Aballah Bacha. He asks if I know his family.

He too studied law—he and one of his bodyguards, Yousef Farsane.
Chartoun? He showed me an official map. Here it is
where the road from Damascus turns before Aleih. Captured
for obvious strategic reasons. At least twelve massacred,

one hundred forty-seven houses and the church destroyed.
I insult him if I don't smoke the Marlboro he offers,
don't drink Scotch whiskey first, before I drink coffee.
He calls the servant, a tall girl from Mauritania.

She became his when he was the Ambassador there, he says.
Lebanon is like Kafka, he says—emphasizing Kafka.
I should get in touch with him when I come to Los Angeles again;
he would like to introduce me to some of his friends.

You say the Shah of Baabda sits like a crow on the head
of the gangster from Syria who kisses both ears of the Sheikh
of Zaghorta, who secretly covets the Prince of Moukharta's access
through State Department intermediaries to the King of Israel—

who cares that your politics change, that you change,
that a sharp nausea plugs your chest, blood quickened
with the harmonies of numbers counted, realized, and forgotten?
It is no time to be uncertain about what has happened or what can.

What has Angele seen? What has she had to put into her brain?
Uncle Shikory's insane; the nuns in the mountain take care of him.
Where is Angele? Gone with the others into the mountain?
Where is Angele? Her eyes were heavy. She wore black ten years.

IN THE BEGINNING WAS LEBANON

In the beginning was Lebanon,
a mountain of musk and the sea
above a star, and the star, Son
of Ali, massacred on a hill
of Galilee grown smooth from rain,
and the rain, oil that washed
skulls and jawbones and pelvises
of children back into red sand
was with God; and the Lebanon
was God. God of high, polished
black boots, faces masked
with black hoods, compounded
of two elements and a single will
to seek vengeance from Abbasids,
Druse, Palestinians, who sits
at the right hand of a swimming
pool in the villa of Saint George
in the kingdom of the Knights
Templar, God who assumes the body
of the father in the holy tomb,
blue-haired or gray-eyed
God who transforms Moslems into dogs
with painted coats, Christians
into slaves with disks in their ears,
God who denies any heart lifted
toward the screen of giant clover,
ignorant God of the great wars
and the families who, reincarnated,
is English and who, beneath
a photograph of Father Abraham,
dozes before bread and sweet milk
above Massar-es-Shouf, this God
who changes tears into bombs
of phosphorus in the eyes of the dumb,
God of the villages named after blood

who, like the sea, sees the houses
at its bottom, who, like the star,
pours down its promises on the Feasts
of the Pigs, who, like fire,
burns the sea and our stomachs
and the brain of the child
who stumbles against the earth around which
brothers and sisters wail.

THAT'S ALL

I work and I remember. I conceive
a river of cracked hands above Manhattan.

No spirit leaped with me in the womb.
No prophet explains why Korean women

thread Atomic Machinery's machines
behind massive, empty criminal tombs.

Why do I make my fire my heart's blood,
two or three ideas thought through

to their conclusions, make my air
dirty the rain around towers of iron,

a brown moon, the whole world?
My power becomes my sorrow.

Truth? My lies are sometimes true.
Firsthand, I now see the God

whose witness is revealed in tongues
before the Exchange on Broad Street

and the transfer of 2,675,000,000 dollars
by tender offer are acts of the mind,

and the calculated truths of First
National City Bank. Too often

I think about third cousins in the Shouf.
I also often think about the fact that

in 1926, after Céline visited
the Ford Rouge foundry and wrote

his treatise on the use of physically
inferior production line workers,

an officially categorized "displaced person"
tied a handkerchief around his face

to breathe the smells and the heat
in a manner so as not to destroy

his lungs and brain for four years
until he was laid off. I don't

meditate on hope and despair.
I don't deny the court that rules

my race is Jewish or Abyssinian.
In good times I transform myself

into the sun's great weight, in bad times
I make myself like smoke on flat wastes.

I don't know why I choose who I am:
I work and I remember, that's all.

WHO TO DENY

I see him before dawn, roused
from sleep by the clatter
of a train over a distant viaduct
and the horns of a freighter
ringing in his ears. I see him
at his job, working volumes
of testimony, fleshing facts.
At the Capitol he argues strategy
to use in opinions
he writes for the Chief Justice,
at lunch at the Grecian Gardens
with Levin—broiled chicken,
fried potatoes, salad—
he agrees: Jimmy Hoffa's body
was sizzled in some warehouse
incinerator in Hamtramck.
Who to deny he knows
annals of businesses out of existence
and his history?—he knows
the number of crimes since 1963.
When she moves her leg to let
her dress above her knee
she catches his eye. Who to deny
he's right there, in the heart of it:
on the bus preoccupied
with his books. Doctor Stavros
prescribes medication
for his pain. Ten years and a war
it takes to learn to ask the price of things
before touching them.
I see him at Grace Hospital.
His father-in-law is dying.
He looks at him, starts to cry—
he cannot attempt to describe.
He helps count what's left behind:

shirts, shoes, documents.
I see him at Saint Anne's. Consciously
taking light from the stained glass,
unashamed to pray—
no act of hope or faith, but to ease
all he doesn't know how to shake.
Later, at the café on Agnes Street,
cup after cup of coffee. Later,
the wind reddens and burns his face.
Later you find him in Grand Circus Park.
The manifesto stuck to the statue
of Mayor Hazen Pingree
of a worker reaching for the sky
against a factory background.
An obscure essay on beauty by Simone Weil
tests him. If you really must know,
he isn't unhappy.

DECEMBER 3, 1937

Not in Budapest beside the powerful dark Danube,
but at a railroad station in a village on Lake Balaton.

A shivering idiot, the moon and the stars witnessed.
Why, when you lay your arm across the track

did you kneel, poet? Cumanian, half Szeklar, half Rumanian
that right arm later found cleanly severed

a hundred feet away from your body mangled
under the wheels of the howling train carrying your freight:

pig snouts and iron and ulcers and greasy dusks
and legs trembling from too much weight.

Why did your women find in your bedroom drawer
a shirt from which you cut off the right sleeve?

Did you believe you would only lose the choice
to pick up a pen again and write? József,

the idiot drooled and giggled when he told how you died,
how your heart burst through your large black eyes.

AN AWFUL LOT WAS HAPPENING

When you come down to particulars everything's more complicated.
Fervent gestures in the South U restaurant, even the Greeks
behind the counter listen. Burned draft cards,
lamb's blood poured over files at the downtown draft board
—acts of resistance, moral values begun.

Saint Augustine in *De Trinitate* didn't see memory structured
by public events. A great moment in my life—not purple clouds
which excited my longings in Nichols Arboretum;
instead, the rumor cancer spread through Lyndon Johnson's brain.
Saint Augustine in his *Enchiridion ad Laurentium* didn't see

her dress and bra across the only chair in my small room
at One Thousand Four Olivia. I couldn't comprehend
whether more words might mean more, my greed, untrained,
not yet certain of its justifications.
And there was war. And from the bluffs above the Huron River

rain of starlight above Ann Arbor's lights, three, four
bell chimes ringing in the Tower. It wasn't Rome.
She dizzied me with excessive desires and thoughts.
What I wanted from all my talk of beauty, she said, was power,
and because of it, she said, I'd cause much suffering.

Although I never bragged misery—maybe once. I was serious.
What was I supposed to do when I heard you could be beaten or
     worse
in the neighborhood in Detroit between Linwood and Dexter,
the color of your eyes wrong. These are facts.
Professor Fuller's response that no one taught them to be quiet.

Glass from the bank's large plated windows all over the street.
I telephoned—line busy; tried again a few minutes later
—no answer. Where is she?—the verge of tears.

Swinburnian dactyls merely went through my ears. Advocated
concision, spatial range, temporal disposition of simple language.

And didn't the spokesman for the Black Action Movement
also receive a number over three hundred in the draft lottery
and attend graduate school? —I came back.
Three years later, every space turned inside out.
January, noon, beams of light across you shake out. Confused,

whirling joy when you slid off me. I leaned
again to embrace you. Uniform Commercial Code on the table.
On the dresser, a cup of coffee, tulips in a vase.
How to explain to myself how much I love you.
In the Law Quadrangle—my peer. He commanded Marines

in the Anhoa Basin. What did I know—what hookworms are like.
What it's like to shoot a Viet Cong, popped from a hole, in the eye.
A piece of metal in your kidney. It's too easy
to be sheep, he concludes, softly. Or too difficult,
I add, softly. He stares at me and whispers something.

When I answered I intended to maintain freedom my brother was
    riled.
What, or who, collides in you beside whose body I sleep?
No work at Tool & Die, Motors, Transmission, or Tractor
while the price of American crude rises another dollar.
There really wasn't enough work anywhere. And there was war

God the spirit of holy tongues couldn't release me from,
or from my dumbness. Pressured—delirious—
from too much inductive thinking, I waited for
the image in whose presence the heart opens and opens
and lived to sleep well; of necessity assessed earth's profit

in green and red May twilight. —You came toward me
in your black skirt, white blouse rolled at the sleeves.
Anticipation of your eyes, your loose hair!
My elementary needs—to cohere, to control.
An awful lot was happening and I wanted more.

I PAY THE PRICE

Memory slipping more and more,
whole days no longer exist.

It's not that I don't feel well.
Pulse 77, 76, I've learned

nothing will pass. Yesterday
the news full of dead,

the *Dictionary on Historical Principles*
open on the table

at the definition of "sentiment,"
today I hear market analysts

expectantly attend the latest
conferences on chaos.

Before the picture window vista
of the East River, I hear Miss

Newman—she insists she be called
Miss—expound her aesthetic.

"This city, the ultimate art!
Masses of steel and light

jutted beyond heaven, a miracle
that is human and works."

This city of my own, dull gray,
rose, yellow, murky pink skies.

I know what I'm saying. I know
tomorrow I may forget

the man whom I see tonight
on Pearl Street under the Bridge

who appears at first to have no head.
He asks me to tell him

who he is, to take him, please,
to the police. He is sick,

mentally. He hasn't controlled
his bladder or his bowels.

Tomorrow I've also a big day ahead of me
protecting interests.

Though I don't have the appropriate letters
to get where I want,

my progress continues.
I distance myself to see myself

say to myself even before
I hang up the telephone, "I love this!"

From my apartment, from which I've a good view
of the same Bridge, I watch

a workman standing on the pier, looking
across at the coast turning toward

the Narrows, his hands bandaged,
victim of a work accident

who doesn't know what to think
or what to do and hasn't enough

to buy himself something to settle his mind.
I walk about my rooms

composing arguments in my defense.
"Live and die before a mirror,"

Baudelaire says, sipping espresso
at the corner of Hudson and Barrow.

I live in words and off my flesh
in order to pay the price.

When the ancient fury persists,
I pay the price.

LET US PRAY

My name is Lawrence Joseph,
in the name of my father,
Joseph, who's also my son,
and in the name of the women

who receive me. I confess
too much. For my penance:
corporal works of mercy.
Who cleansed the prophet Isaias

with a burning coal deign
purify me that I may worthily
proclaim. Let me pray.
At the time the greatest

commandment was to seize
the light, I was light;
in those days innocence
rescued. Let us pray.

We cry from what makes sense.
Our flesh, resurrected,
multiplies and divides
into countless fiery tongues.

Let your cry come to me.
I will not forsake you,
I, Lawrence Joseph, loved so much
by your pain and your beauty.

THE GREAT SOCIETY

Where my mother prayed for my birth
no more confessionals or votive candles
or statue of Blessed Martin de Porres.
A flock of swans above Belle Isle.
Grease in the river and in my hair.

A Great Society, the President declares
in the football stadium eleven miles
from the sign "Welcome to Romulus
Where Healthy Plants Grow." Why
shouldn't my father cheat the wholesaler

to sell to the poor at less loss
or my cousin sing, "Can't forget
the Motor City." On a clear day
the Mayor replaces houses with weeds,
sees the White House. *Bands of roving*

Negro youths, tonight, on Joseph Campau . . .
Szabo crushes beer cans on his skull.
Unskilled labor's wanted at Eldon Axle.
He who soon will need to kill Vietnamese
memorizes Malcolm. After the crowd

outside the blind pig does not disperse
it is difficult to explain to someone
who is not there the 101st Airborne
at the State Fairgrounds, .50-caliber
machine guns mounted on tanks, bazookas.

Brush Street at midnight, the child
huddled with a toy, eerie silence.
Wind brings balm in April, in August
hours of lightning but no rain.
The power of place, the power to demand

an answer from myself, the factories,
the girl whose breasts make me wild,
the communion of saints, streets.
Earth pouring clouds into gray heavens.
Much more violence than I know.

LONDON

Aged malt whiskey and cigarettes
    consumed to enhance consciousness
—read Blake. You can't regulate
    the price of necessaries
without destruction. In a bar
    a few streets from the British Museum
across the table from Oxford's
    latest rising literary star;
not much older than you, his
    history is already impressive.
"There are rules, aren't there,"
    he shrugs, agitatedly,
"and decorum, and irony,"
    he clears his throat and, then,
vanishes behind the Royal Exchange,
    beyond the intent stare
of someone, somewhere, aggrieved
    and the student from the Polytechnic
who laughs after he announces
    he's schizophrenic before he, too,
vanishes down a small lane
    behind the old synagogue
away from where you walk alone
    along Victoria Embankment.
—The sky was low, always low,
    often clear, or raw. You were
the "you" aware of the spite
    and the sorrow. Spirit
to the bone set loose, sensed,
    certain violence. Spirit
in the blood set loose, moved
    by cold smoke from the rows
evaporating. Those whose faces
    thrust forward, gaunt, no chins,

no more eyes—that kind of look
   possessed. It happened;
it wasn't misunderstanding when that woman
   said she never could have
had or have what you have,
   looked away, too sensitive.
An argument on the last train
   from Cambridge to King's Cross
about—the extent of His
   Lordship's estate. The poplar's shadow,
darker than the bluish light,
   spread across complete silence
on the Green at midnight.
   The fact, in Glasgow, straight
razors were means to threaten
   or deter; the fact we are victims
of our truths was true.
   You ought not to have been
what you were, what you
   might have been was a simple fate
in a bag of wind. Nothingness
   erupted. Everything foretold.

ANY AND ALL

You draw nearer to see her more closely,
the blind woman by the bronze doors

of the old Merchants Bank, her mouth
wide open as if in a silent roar,

several dollars stuffed in the pockets
of her mink coat. She is easy to forget

a few days later when you think of her
—not long. The phone is ringing.

You put Byrdman on hold. Polen
wants you in his office immediately.

The lawyers from Mars and the bankers
from Switzerland have arrived to close the deal,

the money in their heads articulated
to the debt of the state of Bolivia.

How much later the Croatian woman
who empties the wastebaskets laughs

when you answer you've been better
and you've been worse. How much sooner

you're told not to tell anyone Byrdman's
grandfather was a Jew. How much No. 54

Wall Street, emblematic reality of extreme
speculations and final effects.

The other evening at a party in the West Sixties
you say as much. None of them knows

what any of it is worth, you say to yourself
later, spitting into an unexpected breeze.

Yellow moons of streetlamps on Ninth Avenue
obscured by atmospheric soot and fog,

in the Twenties empty windows of butcher shops,
factories and warehouses without names,

no taxis, the green light behind the window
of a corner bar. A young man sporting muscles,

a woman he might own on his arm, clearly
doesn't like the way you look or look at him,

lets his leash out enough for his wolf dog
to just nip your leg. Another day

you contemplate your strategy:
think about how they think about you

thinking about them and the look on your face
to prove you have the proper attitude.

Let no laughter reveal moods. Let
Charlotte Stone reveal that her father

over the weekend purchased a peninsula in Rhode Island
for Harry and her, let her teeth

be too large and too gray: there is blood
and there is bloodletting; this is not your blood.

Shut the door and wait. Someone else's father
forgives you when you know not what you do,

reminds you, "He's a weasel but he's my friend."
You're a monkey and you work for him,

decide for him whether his clauses should be restrictive,
whether to replace every "any" with "all."

MY GRANDMA WEIGHED ALMOST NOTHING

It was that April morning that the weight
of tumor mass eroded her frontal bone
through her dura to the brain's substance,

through the corridor of junipers on the road
to Aleih, before the blood of the Great War
dried, and the priest beat Tanous's head

in Hadeth? or was it Chartoun? her cousin
with his large brown, black eyes agreed
and she agreed, in that month of mists,

although Najla burned with whooping cough
and the sun, and mosquitoes ruined the olives,
in that hour of dark blue night, the year

1912 or 1913, wrapped in blankets while sea
turned over toward Marseilles and the island
Ellis became the beautiful valley and the lakes

Ontario and Erie, and the voice on the train
said, Detroit, and she said that word again,
Detroit, before the cold air behind the maples

on Livernois cracked yellow, before Alfred,
in his new suit, bragged Purple Gang
to Angele, in the store on Cass and Temple.

—She couldn't hold herself up, or sleep
and dream dreams she didn't want. She rubbed
her bald skull. My grandma weighed almost

nothing—arms folded around her like sea
and its algae, old sea softened into a Boulevard
or heat or sleep and silence ten times

pain that made her weight her bones
and one or two tears she cried alone
in Women's Hospital that April—then died.

ON NATURE

To proceed: whether results are evident
because they're results. Mists
from chromeplate parts precipitate
ulcers of the skin and cancer.
Raw, hard sun becoming stronger.
Should I save my pity for myself?
Do to others what's been done to you?
Unlimited desires at age thirty-seven
moved to tears before a rose.
It makes sense that the socialist regime
enters into a series of contracts
with private corporations to produce
and market its oil resources.
The data actually prove it's difficult
to draw conclusions on the fate
of the lower middle class. Will
the sophora tree maintain its distinctness?
Free potatoes, trucked from another state,
feeding those reconciled to their doom.
Pork fat? Ten to twenty-four million tons of dust,
loss of light north of the equator,
temperature drop of eighteen to fifty-five degrees
depending on the season. August afternoon
velveted with drink, softened
yellow; floundering marsh, iron river,
blue, heavy air in the bloodstream.
Everyone has some, no one has enough,
but if you have the will you'll be taken care of.
When imported shoes mean the state
of the economy isn't prosperous?
Water with nothing but a little lemon in it.
The woman in bed turning toward
her husband drowsing in a chair?
You get nothing for nothing and a rat's
human as a cat, and the bird

with wild open wings creates a counterlight.
Cool metallic shimmering on the Avenue.
Your eyes I can't take mine from.
Will you love me more if I remain silent?
Even the belief in metamorphosis
after a while doesn't bother me.

THERE I AM AGAIN

I see it again, at dusk, half darkness in its brown light,
large tenements with pillars on Hendrie beside it,

the gas station and garage on John R beside it,
sounds of a cappella from a window somewhere, pure, nearby it

pouring through the smell of fried pork to welcome
whoever enters it to do business.

Today, again, in the second year of the fifth recession
my father holds pickled feets, stomachs, and hearts,

I lift crates of okra and cabbages,
let down crates of buttermilk and beer,

bring live carp to the scale, and come, at last, to respect
the intelligence of roaches in barrels of bottles,

I sell the blood on the wooden floor after the robbery,
salt pork and mustard greens and Silver Satin wine,

but only if you pay, down, on the counter
money you swear you'll never hand over, only if,

for collateral, you don't forget you too may have to kill.
Today, again, in the third year of unlimited prosperity,

the Sunday night the city burns
I hear sirens, I hear broken glass, I believe

the shadow of my father's hand that touches my hair,
my cousin loading a carbine, my uncle losing his mind

today in a place the length of a pig's snout
in a time the depth of a cow's brain

in Joseph's Market on the corner of John R and Hendrie
there I am again: always, everywhere,

apron on, alone behind the cash register, the grocer's son
angry, ashamed, and proud as the poor with whom he deals.

BEFORE OUR EYES

BEFORE OUR EYES

The sky almost transparent, saturated
manganese blue. Windy and cold.
A yellow line beside a black line,
the chimney on the roof a yellow line
behind the mountain ash on Horatio.
A circular cut of pink flesh hanging
in the shop. Fish, flattened, copper,
heads chopped off. The point is to bring
depths to the surface, to elevate
sensuous experience into speech
and the social contract. Ribbons of smoke
silhouette the pier, a navy of yachts
pounded by the river's green waves.
By written I mean made, by made I mean felt;
concealed things, sweet sleep of colors.
So you will be, perhaps appropriately,
dismissed for it, a morality of seeing,
laying it on. Who among the idealists
won't sit in the private domain,
exchange culture with the moneymakers?
Here's one with acute hypertension
ready to crack the pressure cuff,
there's the type whose hallucinatory
devolution of the history of tribes
is personalized. My grandpa? He never
contended where Lebanon's history
began, if the child prince was smuggled
by his mother to a Catholic family
in the Mountain where he passed his boyhood
in his father's religion, a Druse,
the most secret sect of Islam.
I received the news in Jerusalem—
the Beirut Easter radio event, the dancer
undulating to sounds of explosions
outside the studio. The future isn't Africa,

my friend, and Europe's a peninsula of Asia,
and your America's a creation of Europe,
he laughed, the newspaperman, pointing
his finger. Still, don't street smarts
matter? Waiting rooms, shopping centers,
after all, empty moods and emotions.
And no denial's built up inside me.
It was, I admit, more charged than
I thought at the time. More predetermined.
Silver and red scraps inside the air,
cascades of sublimated pig iron.
Language more discursive, a more sequential
expression, and I attested to it.
The old dying? The new not yet born? The old,
the new, you fool, aphorized by Henry Ford
in '22. First make the cars, the roads
will follow. Modes of production created
of their own accord. The process runs
of its own accord. Current and diaphanous
sight and sound, comprehended, but poetry
I know something about. The act of forming
imagined language resisting humiliation.
Fading browns and reds, a maroon glow,
sadness and brightness, glorified.
Voices over charred embankments, smell
of fire and fat. The pure metamorphic
rush through with senses, just as you said
it would be. The soft, subtle twilight
only the bearer feels, broken into angles,
best kept to oneself. For the time being
let's just keep to what's before our eyes.

A FLAKE OF LIGHT MOVED

Sunset, for a while
animated, colors appeared
out of nowhere.
We crossed Cornelia Street,
ate dinner in the open air.

"Love," she observed,
or was it me? I looked around.
Diagonal shadows slid across
one façade after another,
down to the river.

At the table opposite
a deeper blackness.
Something in the contour
of that ebony shape
caught my eye.

A flake of light moved. The great
island intermingling
watery lilac haze. Everyone
watched, as if hypnotized, and more,
much more, than that.

MATERIAL FACTS

On the J train, a gun swung
toward the wide-eyed messenger
with a crippled hand, a burly man
wearing sunglasses tells
witnesses "be cool," the bullet
shattering a window after
ripping the heart apart.
At the Canal Street station,
slowly up the steps, head down,
he's vanished into Chinatown.

Rush hour. Chilled September
morning fresh and red clouds
beaten into purpled
bronze tarnished green. In front of me
another apocalypse is making
gestures, punching in and out,
hat askew on a conical head, ears
pointed like artichoke leaves.
Over there a boy scoots
a dog on a board with wheels.

I'm cool. Another double espresso
and a memory too, possessed
by finesse, a dissociated
sense of the voice of the stranger
who laughs the word "really"
out loud, his designer jacket
covered with zippers, flirting
hard with the woman employed
by the Caffè Giotto. Myself,
self-made, separated from myself,

who cares? That woman wears
a very tiny scripted name

on the chain around her neck.
Something about words and grief
I've forgotten. Something about
words and tears is forgotten.
Note that, on the new jail's wall,
the bas-relief of Confucius
comes off as decoration. See,
people want what you've got,

and, higher up, the visions
are clear: massive, dark blight,
millions with nothing to do;
ministers of every nation
courting financiers the way
the princes of Suzdal used to
kneel before the Golden Horde.
Regulators, assembled, argue
whether the freedom of speech
embraces government computers.

That's that. And this child looks
almost sideways at you,
suspicious, narrow blue face.
Then, grizzled in a tattered coat,
earflap hat and plaid pants,
a star of the screen, after a take,
switches into Popeye the Sailor,
an earlier role, entertaining
those behind the barricade
who laugh and applaud until

reality changes the script.
A child again, who doesn't use
words at all, says something
by slightly turning a corner

of the mouth, hiding material
facts from your perception,
standing beside a carp in a large
iron tank swimming upside down
in the window of Bank Central Asia
on a corner in Chinatown.

ADMISSIONS AGAINST INTEREST

I

Taking my time, literal as I seemed, crazy
enough for silly disputes, actually Asiatically

sorry-eyed, reconciled finally
to the fact the January snow

behind the silver shed was only that,
the sudden sense you've seen it all before

appearing to take shape. For the likes of me
the weather wasn't any theory,

only conflagrations of the specks of a scene,
of rain the smell of smoldering soot,

clouds sweeping crimson down the street,
a physical thing. Bound by the Continual

Ministries of Thine Anger—a funny sight,
on both knees, all or nothing

outside in, wanting evil to disappear,
a complex character rattling off his complexity

the way, in Arabic, my grandmother would.
Mind you, though, my primary rule:

never use the word "I" unless you have to,
but sell it cheaply to survive.

II

Now, what type of animal asks after facts?
—so I'm a lawyer. Maybe charming,

direct yet as circumspect as any other lawyer
going on about concrete forces of civil

society substantially beyond anyone's grasp
and about money. Things like "you too

may be silenced the way powerful
corporations silence, contractually"

attract my attention. The issue's
bifurcated. "Why divide the dead?"

the Foreign Minister asks, "what's one life
when you've lost twenty million?"

And if what has happened during my life
had been otherwise could I say

I would have seen it much differently?
Authority? Out of deeper strata

illuminations. A lot of substance
chooses you. And it's no one's business

judging the secrets each of us needs:
I don't know what I'd do without my Double.

III

So the times demanded figuring out,
and on winter evenings beams of violet

appeared, thin and violent. Gorgeous violet
avenue, gentle, frightened look. The state's agency

assigned to the task of measuring toxicological
effects on the sticky matter

of recollection cells doesn't have any idea.
The air roundabout the Bridge can't be

gold. "You know it makes you want to
shout," the girl on the bus, laughing, shouts,

throws both her hands up, the same song
tuned up on her radio, and I'm off into a mood again,

another internal swoon. So certain combinations
never before are worked on and hard,

knowing early on I could never act
as if I didn't think. My best cogitations

dwell in air so thick it weighs
on the skin, a solid complex, constrained

by this woman's clear fierce eyes wet
in this rain either with rain or with tears.

IV

And so I've had, vast and gray, the sky
my heart, amazed, determined by

the sight of a shimmering simulacrum,
undisturbed color. My admissions

against interest look smaller,
confirmations of another order.

My ancestors are on another plane,
never wholly innocent feeling any horror,

soul-contracted children of common cells,
never wholly distributed sensations

dejected into vertical visions and desire.
So I too am late at my singing,

too much to the point, but now I'm seeing
words are talk and words themselves

forms of feeling, rose-colored splashings
the ice-cold dawn, reliance upon

bare winds pouncing that dot of fire
inside compressed half-luminous air

deflected out of those places I see
formed into feeling, patches of light.

UNDER A SPELL

Now the governor of the Federal Reserve Bank
doesn't know how much more he can take
while my thoughts wander outside me and can't be grasped—
I'm under a spell. While the prisoners
on Death Row whose brain cells will reach
the point of boiling water during electrocution
receive blessings through cable television
and presidents and commissars devise
international housecleanings
history won't recognize for years,
the precedence of language and image preoccupies me too
under the influence of a spell.
Under a spell you have to remember
Monday morning of the insurrection,
the body in the ruins of Stanley's
Patent Medicine Store on John R
a block away from Joseph's Market,
when we argued time and space and memory are the same,
worked at The Rouge or The Axle,
read essays by an activist monk on nonviolence
unaware of the strains we placed on our souls,
skies always choked by gray clouds
moving at different speeds, slag piled
pink and black at the end of the streets.
Under a spell paradise opens again,
a labyrinth. The vistas down the cross streets
are slabs of sun. The confused time
we cried in each other's arms.
Returning at the end of the suffering
to myself who loves no one. Returning
years later to that smoky twilight, still easy to find,
the breezes and sea smells from the Hudson

unexpectedly surrounding us, your eyes
unusually blue. Only you—with whom I can't pretend—
see everything go through me. Nothing's said
when you turn and look through me.

OVER DARKENING GOLD

I

So here we are. Thieves stealing from thieves
in a society of complex spheres,
wondering what you should do. And still
stars blown outside the eye's corner.

II

The babies are asleep in beautiful lines.
But your eye's circuit is going so fast
we're no longer human. In that other place
a dog is still wailing in the background.

III

She said, "That's what I said." She said it.
"Desire isn't a form of sorrow," she said.
Around us wild metallic shimmering,
history, a subject, inside the sky.

IV

Inwards—and backwards, too. The difficult
memory of a divisive memory, killing
the order of the day. The state of the state
consumes the sublime ebony of the moon.

V

Ease up! No, ease down. You're right.
These days one must be especially careful.
The determined are constantly moving,
formed over gold, over darkening gold.

GENERATION
(after Akhmatova)

Matter smashed—Atomic Age America—
accelerated, dawn's desert light
blinding new. Kaiser Aluminum
spouting luminous brass vapors
at the bottom of the steaming valley.
Reality depends on (rumor has it
in The Café Society Downtown)
what you look at. Reality
in the woman's mind: her lover,
before he died, must have seen
a whole city quivering, blossoming
firebombs, pink and bright green.
It depends how you look at it,
phantasmagorical United States;
yet an astute observer perceives
melancholy anger on the faces
of illegal strikers resembles
looks of workers Diego Rivera
cartooned in his Detroit Industry
fresco of the thirties.
    Mildly opaque Indian summer sun
a newly broken painted colt
out of control scents alfalfa
twisted by winds over land not yet
disfigured by bankruptcy. Circling
snow beyond a forested slope
from up above a whirlwind blows
horizontally against an ancient man
walking on ice to fill a house
of titmice with bread and water.
Optimism?—that would suppose
Miami ideas opposed to Chicago
facts; but vision sustains,
a style of seeing: a child catches

sunlight in a pocket mirror,
refracts it into a senator's eyes.
Of course, America contains its grand
gardens, lakes of roses, a monkey on a leash
chewing a pomegranate, glass after glass
of cocaine-pulque, orbits of fear.
Nerves sensitive to orbits of finance
are permitted to express what a girl
in a smelt furnace can't. I know that.
You do too. You know about the zigzagged
plutocratic brain, i.e., increased
incidence of schizophrenia (even back then)
right through the nation. You are too
struck by the state of flux, everything
natural, even the half-comic nature
of the suburbs, democratic views,
oil derricks in front of the State Capitol,
a pubescent boy with diamond molars,
banks named Manufacturers and Republic.
    Allurements, personalized sentiments,
    covenants restricting the sale
    of property to anyone descended
    from anyone born in Africa or Asia,
    hatred of the poor, hatred condensed.
    Goats under observation in Berkeley
    survived Bikini, statue of Jesus
    hands opened miraculously bleeding
    (and those dark deep liquid eyes
    of such color transposed dusk,
    hands strong and soft, wry,
    sad smile, frailty I could not know
    bequeathed by her, my legacy).
    Time, hypertense, turned into breadth
    —a piece of flesh is stuck to a shoe!—

lightning syntax the color of skin
soaring over undifferentiated
difficulty and necessity: a pen's
aqua ink on paper without lines . . .

So that's when we got the idea in our heads
to be born, not to let the sights
slip away, choosing in a badly measured time
human form over nonbeing.

TIME WILL TELL IF SO

A time of comedy sprung
to the eye, a sensational
time of substance and of form,
iridescent existences,
and the same old lowlife.

Go ahead and laugh. Who
needs an imagination?
The thug with a wax complexion
guarantees his audience
you can have anybody killed for

a crate of imported oranges.
Circles of yellow mist
coiled from the open sea,
an old man approaches,
salutes, then walks away.

From one instant to another.
I can't keep my eyes
away from those fingers,
those beams of light
in the middle of the air.

An aura? Time will tell
if so. Alone at a window
lustrous with amber rain,
a figure, realized,
resonates, exhausted by love.

ABOUT THIS

I surfaced from my reflections to see
wartime. YOUR BANK ACCOUNT AND FUCKING COUNT

a sign on the mirror of Le Club Beirut,
an obvious object of interpretation during,

quote, the month that shook the world—
and here and in Paris the fashion news

this season color runs riot. Once again,
in the midst of delirium, my companions

on the subway, those who clean offices
all through the night, close their eyes,

Ash Wednesday–faced, much less anxious,
even more exhausted. That beauty's

green-gray eyes slanting like a cat's
must feel the battery of worldviews.

I do, and believe Nebuchadnezzar in his bunker
religiously is watching himself on Cable

Network News. Where's my sense of humor?
Prices are soaring in the futures pits.

There—over there are the Asian refugees
starting to tear apart the sewage pipes

under the villas to moisten their lips.
Here I squint into the twilight's blazes,

into stabs of dazzling dark radiations,
a set of sights attending my sunbath.

One of us, very old, stops uncontrollably
laughing, sighs, sighs, three, four times,

before starting in again. That rickety one
staring hard at the digital disc player

on display in the World Financial Center's
Palace of Palm Trees covets precision.

Gold (the old favorite in times of stress)
has relinquished its postinvasion gains.

Enough of a shooting war, military
expenditures, there may be no recession.

Is it true, the rumor that the new
instruments of equity are children, commodified?

That the Attorney General has bit off his tongue?
Those are—nails! that maniac wearing

wingtip shoes, turning a tattooed
cheek, throws at us while we talk about evil

outside, over burgundy, at the Cloisters.
This is August and September. This is wartime

bound to be, the social and money value
of human beings in this Republic clear

as can be in air gone pink and translucent
with high-flying clouds and white heat.

WHOSE PERFORMANCE AM I WATCHING?

It's this way, by these words, too much yet still to be proven,
on the table in the café the soft laurel-like leaves,
stamens tinged yellow, outside, inside the winter
like a flash, sky thundered silver, outpourings cold
and distended, indistinguishable from a mood of the mind,
the time of sadness far away. "It's very nice," the father says
to his daughters, seizing a point of light out of the air,
drawing it out, looking hard at it, inhaling a cigarette,
opening and closing his eyes in rapid bursts of feeling.
"Just look!" and I did, and there, on the street, Hudson Street,
a rose-colored woman about to kiss a rose-colored man,
both of them older, under a linden tree, behind them
the elevated absence you've learned to let be. I've never
forgotten the expression on their faces, the only
human beings I've ever seen without that rapacious look
everyone else is possessed by. Brightness streaming in every
direction. Judgment, desire, sentence structure taking place.
Not in Siena, but right here, the spokes of the streets
                    suffused by color.
In a nearby bar the youths, including the victims, members,
                    Born to Kill gang,
involved in a fatal argument over a cellular phone,
                    a Malaysian woman.
There, nevertheless, may be more to the story, after all
                    the exalted rooms,
the Board of Directors, the future determined
                    a long time ago.
Exactly how much one poet's thinking has influenced
                    what's in the air
—a veteran of a foreign war is washing his hands
                    with imaginary soap,
whistling the tune of the Contra War video. I enjoy
                    a good laugh too
at the old comic business. But once again the lure is there,
                    everything accepted

hits you in the eye. Illustrated magazines burning on
the Brooklyn Bridge.
No peace nor lack of peace, only the haze of a form. It occurs
to me the girl in an overcoat sitting alone is listening to
herself, eyeing me with an uncertainty that isn't malevolent.
The dancer in the shiny leather jeans says Europe's more subtle.
I'm sorry, I know, it's a private matter, I wouldn't let go
until late at night, my thoughts absorbed ever since.
"No, it is"—the famous member of the international press
gang mocked—"the truth. First Islam, then the Chinese,
then what do you think?" There I am, out of my depth,
in a kind of fire-green, confusing the words you and I,
taken still by the physical silence of your hands. My God,
my God, whose performance am I watching? Wouldn't I have to
do it all anyway for the sake of the child turned blue?
The current mood also changing, whatever it is, opaquely
composed and overwrought attenuation moved through floating
planets of space, dusted by stars. This situation.
On St. Luke's Place the tree edges melting. You feel
the river's cold. The filtered sunlight insinuating opulence.

SENTIMENTAL EDUCATION

So no self-centered anarchism
was of use, too manic the sense
of economy, employment and inflation
curved. Detroit's achromatic
sky for a son of lower
middle class parents like me
glowed. My baptism by fire
in the ancient manner,
at my father's side in a burning city,
nothing sacramental about it.

Everything was—everything fast!
Strips of twilight shadow sheened
transparency and cast
a concisely stylized groove
you could count on
around the door to the dance.
War days conscientiously objected to,
the racial on me all the time,
I knew my place, you might say,
and white-hot ingots

in their molds, same time,
same place blue jays among the marigolds
held their own beside
the most terrible rage, tears wept
for no reason at all except
what might have been
—my mother's tears, for instance.
She doesn't sleep well
in this climate
composed of pale tints.

But first, back to Henry Ford.
Of the world-famous Highland Park Plant

Otto Moog, the German engineer,
in 1923 proclaimed (Vladimir
Lenin thought so too): "No symphony
compares to the music hammering
through the colossal workplace"
—proof, so to speak,
that speech propels the purposes
by which it's been shaped.

But back, first, to Marvin Gaye,
during an interview in Brussels.
"Remember the Turbans?" he asks,
laughing at the memory. "Cats
sported silk headdresses, sang up
a storm. Had this one hit tune,
'Please Let Me Show You Around Myself,'
the lyrics comparing enclosed
empty space to an open heart
showed me to appreciate language."

Back to, because you want to,
Grand Boulevard, excessive sky
hot and indigo, poured out
onto Hendrie. Inside the store,
Grandpa lifts you into his arms,
small as a single summer Sunday,
a kind of memory trance truly
dark, deep and dark, steel dark,
not as pure, but almost as pure,
as pure unattainable light.

What now? The palette's red.
The beggars wear red in their hair.
Red's contained in the place's currency.
The distance sustained between

subject and object looks red.
History, increasingly ephemeral,
is red. The switches of the music are
red while you mark the beat,
consistent with your education,
without any inner dispute.

OUT OF THE BLUE

Not that we lacked experience.
We simply had no talent for murder.
And then it was November again.

The air brisk and cold, lights clicked
softly in a burnished glow.
A world with its own wild system of desires.

Yet somehow more fragile.
In a completely different place
from its syntax, in fact—far ahead of it.

And who could not be struck by the notion?
A Great Wheel, gold and gray,
out of the blue, burst in flame.

Taking the shape of the moment.
Disappearing
in a crevice in the sky.

BROODING

How could I foresee
looking back seven
centuries, one rose
in the crystal vase
in the room where
she stood before me,
legs slightly apart,
golden dusk all over us
when she insisted
not to go on talking
as if I was dreaming,
arguing the *Summa
Theologica*'s proofs
that God is the love
she was brought up on,
she and I. Always
this point of departure
always, ceaselessly,
pushed toward
particulars of light
insistent emotions
sometimes abstracted
rarefied air.
Not at all fazed
that man on Grand Street
is yelling, "Eloi,
eloi, lama sabachthani,"
I've heard the words
before. Blocks away
substance dealers
finance insurance
companies, purchase
pension funds.
Russia, I see, once again
appearing in

our minds. A conversation
at a private reception
for the recent celebrity
intellectual
of the almost freed
state—"No one," he
laughs at my inquiry,
"reads Mayakovsky
anymore." But, decidedly,
more astute than
the anarcho-capitalist
lawyers he easily
convinces what lies
deep in his heart
—a bag of the softest
leather, with many
zippers, on his shoulder.
Perhaps he knows
how perfectly
he mimics a southern
Californian—"Paradise is
a fuck-dance
to the rhythms on video
of electronically
sexual dollars"
—while here I am feeling
sorry for him,
soul sickness
which has, like our own
strabismic know-how,
caused the species
dementia praecox
in the corners of various
chancelleries;
with all due respect

the soul brother
hasn't yet entertained
certain elegantly
styled arrangements,
transmogrified servitudes
no one believes.
God, but who could
conceive it all?
Excessive cerulean
winds consecrated
green, feeling in
the back of the neck
a kind of mingling,
a nearness from far away,
and the finest flower
of the nation's
executive branch,
frazzled and fatigued
before the press
under April showers
in Memphis, Tennessee,
wondering out loud,
"There's no way
I can explain how
I came to be here"
—quickly brushed
permanence around
further fact:
in Bose-Einstein physics
past and present
generate wave
functions on
consciousness equal
to a laser beam's time.
What you see,

not what you do,
what we say is absolutely
modern. What
do I see? A baby's
mysterious inability
to open his eyes.
What do I do?
Mysteriously
a month-old baby
can't open his eyes.

VARIATIONS ON VARIATIONS ON A THEME

I

Winter dragged on. Established remnants
fell apart, displaced by chaos, by functions.
Take the renowned banker who's murmuring
the socialization of money has become
an abstract force and he's nervous.
In the background, out of the ground of being,
a resident of the Hill, in her tin hut
at the end of the Manhattan Bridge, insists
she possesses a master's degree in English.

II

My friend the priest is studying Malcolm's
X, how Detroit Red decided to redesign
his sorrow—"the X a cross," he contends,
though none of it the gnosticism popularized
in certain circles. The way my friend
sees it, the species is undergoing
a cerebral mutation three distinct types
will survive: those who need to kill,
those who wait silently for transformation,
and those, the militants, seesawing
between the murderers and the victims.

III

Tell me about it! Molten copper
burned copper into an ethereal haze.
"My God," she added softly, "it seems
so terribly long ago." No, this afternoon,
I actually saw one of my peers
pour perfume over the body of a shadow.

IV

And that's the law. To bring to light
most hidden depths. The juror screaming
defendant's the devil staring at her
making her insane. The intense strain
phrasing the truth, the whole truth, nothing
but sentences, endless sentences.

V

I haven't forgotten. The way you converse
—to attend once more to words as words.
I mean it. Lips and skin remember, a voice
on the Avenue sensuous enough to touch.

VI

Gesticulating his head forward, poking
his baby finger, intonations arising
in a manner of speaking without agitation,
he says to her he doesn't understand
metempsychosis. In Walt Whitman's country,
pink and turquoise rhododendrons are
like porcelain after the rain, square,
dark-blinded windows behind her eyes,
hazel and hard, relenting at moments,
bound at the corners by minuscule lines.

VII

The war is a few days old. In the ever-blue
the sun continues its journey. You won't
kill their love of the actual. Let them go
conquer the world, march with Alexander:
there is Ur, the Chaldean city, a bronze
flake on a rock; there are millions, millions
plunged and numbed by dreams of blood.
It was then I had an attack of madness

—the eyewitness account the vanquished
appeared as if from a mirage of hot
oily smoke in search of someone
to surrender to—which almost made me smile.

VIII
What are you saying? This light is famous,
its sad, secret violet, and, this evening,
West and East rivers turned into one.
To remember and imagine at the same time
—that was the month of June that year.
Within the intensity you showed me
both cloudiness and transparency can be painted.

IN A FIT OF MY OWN VIVIDNESS

In a fit, you might say, of my own vividness,
feeling January's crystal cold light,
a kind of—what's the precise phrase?—
bias on my part.
It's hard to throw off what you're subject to.
Examining it closely, the house in Royal Oak,
a mother's footsteps in the hallway, her body
shaking, space and time she won't realize
in incessant distress. You think about a thing
like that. The Palm Sunday procession
halfway through the century, Christ Resurrected
painted on our candles. Yellows on yellows.
Codes in effect. Limitless
marketplace assumed
transcendence. Something or other
tempted fate. So much for a family market
reduced to the poverty line
by a freeway. Time opaque and nullifying
perspective materialized. Those years my father
cut meat for the Great Atlantic & Pacific Tea Company
(knew to slice away the sinewy nerves), working
at the other store a few nights a week for his brother.
It was hot. There was smoke. It was hell.
Fire stuck together earth and sky, broken glass,
blood on the streets, berserk not only on Asian
battlefields, those events never transubstantiated
the shades disturbed. While the perpetrator raged
into spasms, the automatic shot off, the bullet
surfaced (after turning in the hospital bed my father
said, "There's lead in my ass"). Some thousand
sixteen-hour workdays before you're sublime.
Sorting out, at a minimum, the issue changes
and moods do too. Your mother worrying anyway,
her name whispered over and over again to herself

in the kitchen. The Medical Consultation Report:
"multi-infarct dementia, left and right hemispheres."
Don't you raise your voice! No—did you think so?—
not tears! This discord enacts no measure.

AFTER ALL

The truth of knowing,
the absolute of feeling
—those were your
words—what we know.

A distance that never
gives way. The grandeur
this side of heaven
must be immense, after all.

And just as well to
keep still evening's
gray velvet ricocheted
across the street.

SOME SORT OF CHRONICLER I AM

Some sort of chronicler I am, mixing
emotional perceptions and digressions,

choler, melancholy, a sanguine view.
Through a transparent eye, the need, sometimes,

to see everything simultaneously
—strange need to confront everyone

with equal respect. Although the citizen
across the aisle on the Number Three

subway doesn't appreciate my respect.
Look at his eyes—both of them popping

from injections of essence of poppy;
listen to his voice bordering on a shrill.

His declaration: he's a victim of acquired
immuno-deficiency syndrome. His addiction

he acquired during the Indo-Chinese war.
Specified "underclass" by the Department of Labor

—he's underclass, all right: no class
if you're perpetually diseased and poor.

Named "blessed" by one of our Parnassians
known to make the egotistical sublime

—blessed, indeed; he's definitely blessed.
His wounds open, here, on the surface:

you might say he's shrieking his stigmata.
I know—you'd prefer I change the subject

(I know how to change the subject).
Battery Park's atmosphere changes

mists in which two children play and scratch
like a couple of kittens until the green

layers of light cover them completely,
a sense of anguished fulfillment arising

without me, beauty needled into awareness
without me, beauty always present in

what happened that instant her silhouette
moved across the wall, magnified sounds

her blouse made scraped against her skin
—workers, boarded storefronts, limousines

with tinted windows, windows with iron bars,
lace-patterned legs, someone without legs,

merged within the metathetical imagination
we're all part of, no matter how personal

we think we are. Has anyone considered
during the depression of 1921

Carlos Williams felt a physician's pain,
vowed to maintain the most compressed

expression of perceptions and ardors
—intrinsic, undulant, physical movement—

revealed in the speech he heard around him
(dynamization of emotions into imagined

form as a reality in itself).
Wallace Stevens—remember his work

covered high-risk losses—knowingly chose
during the bank closings of early '33

to suspend his grief between social planes
he'd transpose into thoughts, figures, colors

—you don't think he saw the woman beneath
golden clouds tortured by destitution,

fear too naked for her own shadow's shape?
In 1944, an Alsatian who composed

poems in French and in German, exiled
for fear of death in a state-created camp—

his eye structure, by law, defined as "Jewish"—
sensed the gist. Diagnosed with leukemia,

Yvan Goll gave the name Lackawanna
Manahatta to our metropolis—Manahatta

locked in Judgment's pregnant days, he sang,
Lackawanna of pregnant nights and sulfurous

pheasant mortality riddled with light
lying dormant in a shock of blond hair

half made of telephones, half made of tears.
The heavy changes of the light—I know.

Faint sliver of new moon and distant Mars
glow through to Lackawanna Manahatta.

Above a street in the lower Nineties
several leaves from an old ginkgo tree

twist through blackish red on golden air
outside a fashionable bistro where a man

with medals worn across a tailor-cut suit
chides a becoming woman half his age.

"From now on, my dear," he says with authority,
"from now on it's every man for himself."

LINES IMAGINED TRANSLATED INTO A FOREIGN LANGUAGE

And then the logic of war
    succeeded the night
the day bright lemon
    winter sky thinned
to cold peach
    no visible polestar
at the horizon's end
    the Sea of Samarra
outlined before us
    a breach of Asia Minor
incandescent before us
    —"These are the opening
rounds of this war"—
    Fire Specialists
anonymously delirious
    journalists on
the bridge of the *Wisconsin*
    bound by rules
mutating and returned
    into violence.
And I? Am I mad
    or maddened imagining
those who can't
    imagine this return
into violence? No
    tears, we hear,
no sense of terribleness
    or sorrow, nothing
only immense excitement
    when the attack
begins, blocks of light
    suddenly flattening
arc of laser-guided
    purple-tinged halos
around the open night.

Every bomb seems to be
hitting. Explosions
      weirdly traced
lapis lazuli.
      Bridges still standing,
bridges over the Tigris
      River still there—
no action at all
            in the city.
Look at this! This is
      a flash of light
which seems—it seems
      to have come across
north to south close to
      the Al-Rasheed Hotel
before it goes—almost
      like a shooting star.
Or is it? This is
      the imperium
emanating from the District.
      He didn't want to go
into the Service,
      his mother says,
but would help her out,
      do better than the streets,
go to school. Although
      you think you
could be distressed
      by it, don't you? See
—those who proclaim
      myths of predetermined
superiority. Remember
      —the Sykes-Picot Agreement,
wasn't it? Nerve-racking
      the evidence

widespread public
    fragility and debt
overhanging inventory
    and armaments—but for
the realities
    the litanies seem only
to exhaust us. Rule
    by extended clans,
circles of racketeering
    oligarchies abstracted
by—abstractions!
    Mesopotamia's imperial
eminence around 2250
    B.C. overlapping
Egypt's disintegrating
    unities the spectrum
through which events
    multiply and become
—hallucinations!
    Don't worry: the children
will define themselves
    by their age at the time
of this war. Meanings
    imagined into the types
of verbal progression
    a corporate economy
sustains, the language
    of direct expression
subverted by exhaustion,
    not a result
of diminished anguish
    but how it's imagined.
"Look," al-Fekaiki, member,
    Revolutionary Command

Ba'ath Party Rule
 '63, says again, waving
his fork over dinner
 in Paris, "maybe he is
out of his mind or crazy
 or maybe he wants
to die a hero."
 "Play by the rules, though—"
she who wears a diamond
 on her thumb is quoted
saying—"no one bombed
 ever forgets it."
By way of contrast, taxi
 drivers are demanding
up to six thousand
 dollars cash to ferry
outsiders into Jordan.
 This is different:
so delicate the Embassy
 refuses to acknowledge
it's happened. An infant
 in Haifa suffocated
resisting her parents'
 efforts to fasten
her gas mask. I waited
 up all night for it.
A weather front moved
 through the area. Skies
cleared partly today,
 clouds, copper blue
shaded clouds again Sunday
 into the early part
of next week. Repeat it
 one more time, I'll

figure out the meaning,
    then I don't want to
talk anymore.
    In London, the Foreign
Office disclosed
    a report Mr. Hussein's
wife and children
    traveled to Mauritania
aboard three or four
    stolen Kuwaiti
airliners recently painted
    the colors of Iraqi
Airways. In a dispatch
    from Abidjan,
Ivory Coast, Reuters
    says an aide
to Mauritanian President
    Ould Sidi Taya
officially dismissed
    the report as "ridiculous."

JUST THAT

I

So that's it? Just that? No dream.
A memory, and it happened
a while ago. On Grove Street
a sophora tree slightly swayed,
soul to soul in the plum-misted chill.

II

You wait and see. That language doesn't work
anymore, its century is over. It turns out
Joseph's Market is as free as the boy with one arm
kissing the tangerine my father gives him.
The entire place—upside down. Only money
and credit move around, part of the future.

III

So I take another look at my circles,
see them through an aphorism or two.
You do what you do, and do what you must.
There's refuge in observation.
And never expect to make hard cash from a poem.

IV

Actually, the whole night's slow
snow embodied the autoworks'
dull yellow grasses, embankments,
the sweepings. The noisy chains on
Jefferson Avenue, that steamship whistle
blowing beyond Belle Isle,
heaven, in its way, rained justice.
The city rioting seems to have remained
more than a portion of the brain.
The place continues, a state of flux,
opera neither tragic nor comic.

V

His finger jabbing like a revolver,
a talking head in a high-backed chair,
His Honor suddenly takes his glass eye out,
places it on the bench. The Public
Defender's case, he laughs, is a "mystical
allegation." He is, after all, a lawyer.
He can measure what a word means.
In a prison suit the accused smiles, too,
when a point is made in his favor.

VI

What time is it? There's a taxi on the way
downtown. Sulfurous yellow's hot sweet
rose, furious counterpoint, gentle anxiousness,
and words reveal it: gold-pink, sun-shot,
wave-cord, green-gathered. Say no more.
It's there. Except to plead you begin
again, as soon as possible, beautiful secrets,
part of my element, out of mind, in the flesh.

A PARTICULAR EXAMINATION OF CONSCIENCE

Awakened by your body, in the first place,
against mine, sweet and frenzied
skreekings and trillings of starlings
on the fire escape, and a rose sky.
Succumbed again to my gluttonous
appetite for the paper:
the front-page headline DELUSION,
BENIGN AND BIZARRE, RECOGNIZED AS COMMON;
the rumor Chrysler and Allied-Signal
decided to purchase General Motors
publicly denied by the spokesman whose quip
"We're going to buy Greece, instead"
panicked the jittery market.
This morning, thoughts of long ago,
the Gare de l'Est, the last time I saw her,
she was leaving for Berlin and farther.
This morning remembered, the first time in years,
Saint Ignatius's rule:
nothing exists except through the senses
(amid poisons from Bayonne blown
over the harbor). Too much time this afternoon
spent plotting against my enemies.
Crisscrossing the Brooklyn–Queens Expressway,
cool gusts broken into rapid spaces,
one of my sorrows suddenly eased.
Beside me a worker driving a Fury
appeared exhausted, plastic dice
wrapped around his rearview mirror,
above us on the Division Street overpass
a boy bowing, bowing and praying.
Late afternoon conversation with—
I told him he talks the way Seneca would.
Constantly comparing, meditative
yet impersonal style—a moralist.
Computerized systems reduce decisions

to make total war to instants;
absolute speed equals instantaneous
terror, though billions can't read
—I had to tell him to lower his voice.
Imagination split forever—one side
fear, the other hope; no one knows
how to decide, even within oneself.
On Worth Street at twilight delicate
silver light struck through my spine.
Before the courthouse on Centre Street
a barefoot woman danced in a circle.
By force of emotion, the entire day,
thresholds between us more than we know.
Which wounds transformed by which acts of will?
Not crying, not laughter, the howling
tonight on Water Street doubtlessly
contradicted, doubtlessly raving.

MOVEMENT IN THE DISTANCE IS LARGER UP CLOSE

Apart from that, the sun came around
the same time. A certain splendor emerged
illusory and frail, like a rainbow.
Around where we were standing everything
suffused apricot brightness. Even the man
alone in the Café Fledermaus, his table
covered by an old salmon-pink *Financial Times*,
feels he's metering his thoughts, gesturing
as if speaking. These curved lines,

so many images, but I suppose it's necessary to observe again
the rest of it split all over the place, one part
like money, forever within the daily routine, another,
mixing suavity, fragments of harmonic nuances
reflective at the same time abstract and grounded by the beat,
under the influence of connoisseurs of rhythm,
not afraid of being blue, brain on fire from time to time,
longing intensified to the point of—yes. I hear
you. Your absence more palpable than your presence.
And me? I'm often short of breath these days.
But, then, so are the philosophers, whose problems are
the politicians' now. For example, that man you've seen
on television, the head of state who bunches his nails
onto his lips, throwing them outward as if under
the pressure of some invisible bouquet magically forced
out of his mouth, clacking his tongue, proclaiming
the inevitability between Kazakhstan and the Sudan;
and there are many new Americas to discover.
I don't know about you, but it all goes through my skin.
Like the woman over there coughing into the pay phone.
Enlightenment? I've got mine, you've got yours—then what?
I know a prophet who possesses the power of thought transference,
addresses women mostly, recently seen carrying an olive branch.

But can't you see eventually we will be forced to acknowledge
countless children possess an alien language, face it,

get down! The hype alone's no beautiful thing.
What's sold: used shoes to those who prove
indigency. Hot and spicy pork for the ego.
Vodka for pleasure, votive candles to the Virgin.
What's bought: this displaced child, hugging
a kneeling woman, about to ascend into limbo.
So you rampage within yourself—you think
you should be thanked for it? In history's optic
movement in the distance is larger up close.
This is no proverb. Of course I remember
that day—boundless happiness and joy.
The leaves in the park deep, irascible mauve.
The crippled unemployed drawing chalk figures
on the Avenue. Precisely. Where we ought to be.

NOW EVENING COMES FAST FROM THE SEA

The East River looks as black
as the Brooklyn Bridge's shadow.

Thinking back—but those days
are over! A darkening green

conceals the Heights, quivering
twilight cold. I can't

be alone. And yet, somehow
or other, in spite,

or because of you transposed
in the treble of light

that lingers where the music
remains, a great and nuanced

diamond sheet projects itself
at the end of the street,

against the sky. So, still,
refracted into depths,

all beauty isn't underlined;
indignant and ironic

events blocked on top of one another,
dislocations debited

to anamorphosized tribes, city
drawn, caressed, into

circles—do you follow me?
Now evening comes fast from the sea.

OCCIDENT-ORIENT EXPRESS

East and west, converged expression,
analytical instincts, erupted harmonies:
all night a blind woman listens alone
to the radio. And in Tokyo Madame Lenine's
grandniece eats air-blown tuna
pungent as caviar. What do I mean?
Language means. And Jerusalem hangs
mystical in lavender sky
while outside Bethlehem the prophet Elijah's
seen entering a UFO.

Straining to catch the light again,
colorless light, bunches of violets,
a proud, shy woman silently sipping tea.
The process of logical association
you can't escape: the taxi driver
flashes his teeth, "It's in the eyes,
you have to break the other's eyes."
But if you love to hear a heartbeat
you won't sleep well alone. At noon
parts of the world are black with sun.

Or this rumor out of Lebanon:
Party of God regulars taught to kill
by Vietnam War veterans from Las Vegas.
The People's Republic programmatically
nullifies half its language.
The Isle of Dogs's rumor the Prime Minister's
capillaries are quickened
by daily doses of electricity
—reservoirs of the impulse
to work something out every place.

Or this: Moscow, coveting cash, visits Bonn.
Before the bust of Adenauer on the Rhine

a vista appears in the Chairman's mind:
a bright nation cleft with roses
swaying in yellow and flame.
"Where there's a will
there's a way," he assures his bankers
in English, almost singing;
a priapism of form
everyone present giggles at.

Against my heart I listen to you
all the time, all the time.
Against my brain, more visible than dream,
the present's elongations spread
blue behind the fragrant curves
pure abstractions blast through
a fragile mind in a flapping coat
descending the Memorial's steps
toward incalculable rays of sun
set perpendicular into the earth.

INDEX OF TITLES